EVERYDAY PRAYERS

— FOR —

PATIENCE

Giving Yourself and Your Kids the Grace to Grow

BROOKE McGLOTHLIN

WHITAKER
HOUSE

Everyday Prayers for Patience
Giving Yourself and Your Kids the Grace to Grow

www.millionprayingmoms.com
brookemcglothlin.net

ISBN: 979-8-88769-002-5
eBook ISBN: 979-8-88769-003-2
Printed in Colombia
© 2023 by Brooke McGlothlin

Whitaker House
1030 Hunt Valley Circle
New Kensington, PA 15068
www.whitakerhouse.com

Library of Congress Control Number: 2023935337

1 2 3 4 5 6 7 8 9 10 11 **ЦJ** 30 29 28 27 26 25 24 23

CONTENTS

PART TWO: WE CAN BE PATIENT BECAUSE OF WHO THE LORD IS

FOREWORD

I believe the conversation went something like this:

"Hey Brooke, what is the next *Everyday Prayers devotional* based on?"

"The next one is on patience. Do you want to write it?"

"No way," I said. "I wouldn't write that if you paid me a million dollars. So who is writing it?"

"I am," Brooke said with a slight smile.

"Girl, I'm going to pray for you."

I have a hunch that you might be thinking of one or two things right now. First, you might be thinking that I am less than spiritual for refusing to write this beautiful book you now hold in your hands. Or you might be thinking we could totally be best friends and grab coffee together to pray for Brooke and wonder what she was thinking when she agreed to write a book about praying for patience.

All kidding aside, I can tell you what Brooke was thinking because I happen to know her pretty well. She was thinking, *Man, I needed this devotional sixteen years ago when I was a young mom raising two small boys and just trying to get through the day.* She tends to write books that she wished she had herself at one point or another. And whenever she does, they end up being special because she puts her whole heart into it. This one is no different. I can almost guarantee that if you start on day one and stick with it for the next thirty days, you will see a significant change in your life for the better. I can also almost guarantee you will also be tested along the way.

How do I know this? Honestly, it is the same reason I didn't volunteer to write this devotional myself. It happens to be found in a couple of verses in Romans:

> *And not only that, but we also boast in our afflictions, because we know that affliction produces endurance, endurance produces proven character, and proven character produces hope.*
>
> (Romans 5:3–4)

Do you see the word *endurance* above? Endurance is another word for patience. In fact, in *The Message* translation (MSG), the words used for endurance are *"passionate patience."* I'm not sure I would ever describe my patience as passionate—and don't get me started on the idea of rejoicing in suffering. But I can tell you from personal experience that God produces this type of patience through hard seasons of suffering we'd rather skip. I can't entirely say why that is the case, but it appears to be God's way. I'm guessing you may have heard it said that God's ways are not our ways. This is one of the truths we have to accept and simply trust, knowing His ways are best even when we wish with all our impatient hearts that it was otherwise.

Maybe you picked up this book because you are a big Brooke McGlothlin fan, and you read every word she writes. You can count me as part of that club. (See, our coffee date is getting more fun by the minute.) Or maybe you grabbed this book because your patience is less than thin. You are tired of losing it, feeling frustrated, and finding your heart running anxiously after every single fear that rears its ugly head. Me too, friend.

Can I redirect your attention to that gut punch of a verse that I mentioned from Romans? Here is the promise it holds: at no place in that verse does God stop on you. He keeps working and moving and sustaining you as you walk or crawl through suffering. And in the process, He produces patience, then character, and then hope. Now hope is something we all want and something I know an awful lot about. It seems patience and hope have a sweet connection. They are forged in the hard places where God's grace is thick.

I can't think of a better person to walk with you through this journey than Brooke. She is honest, kind, and willing to go first. You are much better off having her words for the next thirty days than mine. And truthfully, I'll be sitting right here with you, wiping away the tears, praying these prayers, and thanking Jesus that His patience with me is the reason I have any hope at all.

See you on the other side my friend.

—Stacey Thacker
Author of *Threadbare Prayer:*
Prayers for Hearts that Feel Hidden, Hurt, or Hopeless

INTRODUCTION

ON PATIENCE

"Give them the grace to grow out of this."

Those words are written on a sticky note that stays permanently attached to my computer monitor. I see it every morning and glance at it off and on throughout my workday. It was meant to be a reminder about giving my children grace as they mature and grow, but it applies to every single relationship I've ever had—family, ministry, school, community, you name it. We are all growing, and God is at work in our lives every moment of every day. The problem is that sometimes people don't grow as fast as we'd like, and God doesn't always act when we think He should.

In my work at Million Praying Moms, I've had the opportunity to run a lot of online gathering spots for large groups of women who are, at the beginning, complete strangers. The majority of these women are believers, but they come from all walks of life and different Christian denominations. They have all been walking with the Lord for differing lengths of time.

Know what that means? There are women in the groups who are very mature in their faith. They've been through the mountains and valleys during the course of their walks with Christ and have hard-earned trust in, and deep knowledge of, His character. But there are also women in the groups who are new to the faith. Their relationship with Jesus is fresh and sweet, but they don't know the Scriptures very well, and they haven't been walking with the Lord long enough to be saturated in His Word. They haven't yet had the opportunity and privilege of having their eyes opened by the Lord, and it shows in what they say and how they respond in the group.

In the beginning, this was problematic. The seasoned believers were hard on the new Christians, and the latter just couldn't relate to the former.

When I realized this, I started to begin every group with these words: "Please remember that as Christians, we all mature at different rates. There will be Christians in this group who are behind you on the journey and Christians in front of you. Give grace." Somehow, this simple reminder is all that's needed to create a more peaceful gathering. I've even seen mature believers take newer Christians under their wing, helping them grow in their faith instead of berating them for taking too long to grow into it.

The word *patience* means the capacity to accept or tolerate delay, trouble, or suffering without getting angry or upset. This, in my opinion, sounds a lot like my life as a parent! How many times a day is our patience tested by someone else or the situation? Fifty? A hundred? More? During the last school year, my son needed me to bring some medicine to him at school. He had broken his finger playing basketball, and the pain medicine we gave him at home that morning hadn't lasted through the entire day. Because of the school rules, I had to halt my workday, drive to the school with a new bottle of medicine, and fill out paperwork.

The first few minutes of the drive, I grumbled and complained, but quickly, the Holy Spirit stopped me and reminded me that I *get* to do this for my kids. My husband and I have intentionally crafted a life that allows me to stop what I'm doing and take care of their needs. It's a privilege. It's what I wanted. And there will be a day when they won't need me in the same way. That, for me, puts patience in parenting in an entirely different perspective.

An old joke goes like this, "Don't ask God for patience. He'll answer by testing yours." To some degree, this is true. I don't know that God is sitting around in heaven just waiting to test our resolve, but parenting, and the Christian life itself, is fundamentally built on trusting something we can't always see…a master plan that reveals itself little by little and often takes turns we can't predict. I'll be honest, just writing this prayer journal makes me a little nervous about what God is going to teach my own family about patience!

We have not arrived. My sweet family is a work in progress just like yours. Promise. Just this morning, over breakfast before school, I was talking to my two sons about Psalm 16:11. The first part of the verse says, *"You [God] reveal the path of life to me."* Both of my sons have recently experienced disappointment. Something happened they had hoped wouldn't or didn't happen that they hoped would. I started the conversation by asking them, "How often do we allow outside circumstances to control how we feel?" After thinking about it for a moment, they both agreed that this is true most of the time. Then I read Psalm 16:11 to them and asked if they believed God's plans for them were good, and that He would do as He promised, making those plans—or paths for their lives—known to them.

It was a good reminder that even when things don't make sense, are delayed, come with trouble, or bring suffering, God's plans are still good, and we can have faith that He'll show us which way to go at just the right time. Even if we choose to take a wrong turn, God, like my GPS, will recalculate the path and still get us where we need to go. He uses everything, even our disobedience, along the way.

My husband closed the conversation by remarking, "So then we don't really need to dwell on it when something doesn't go our way, or someone hurts us, or we made a bad decision. We just have to have patience. We don't have to let those things determine how we feel about ourselves because we know that our God is still directing our paths."

Exactly.

We could wish that we had all the knowledge of God, all of the wisdom we need to do life and bring glory to Him, and knew how to perfectly parent our kids just the right way without having to be patient, but that just isn't the way God designed it. We were born with a purpose, but like it or not, our purpose isn't always about getting to a finish line. It's about living today, right now, in each experience parenting and life bring with the perspective that says, "God is leading me, and He isn't finished. What can I learn from this experience that will keep my family on the right path and bring glory to Him?"

And *that* requires patience.

Let's spend the next thirty days together in study and prayer, asking God to help us see His heart for the way we live and parent our children and develop our patience muscle so that our lives and theirs can be beautiful reflections of His great patience with us. The first fifteen days will help us to personally have a stronger definition of what biblical patience is, while the remaining fifteen days will help us understand God's character better so that we can trust His perfect timing in our lives and in those of our children.

Together,
Brooke McGlothlin

THE THINK, PRAY, PRAISE
METHOD OF DAILY PRAYER

When I first started praying for my own children, I was inspired by two important truths about God's Word:

1. *For the word of God is living and effective and sharper than any double-edged sword, penetrating as far as the separation of soul and spirit, joints and marrow. It is able to judge the thoughts and intentions of the heart.* (Hebrews 4:12)

2. God declares, *"So my word that comes from my mouth will not return to me empty, but it will accomplish what I please and will prosper in what I send it to do"* (Isaiah 55:11).

If those two verses were true—and I believed they were—then it seemed to me that there could be no better thing to pray than God's Word itself! Because this experience was so deeply profound for me, it's the same one I've used to teach other women to pray. I call it my "Think, Pray, Praise" method. It isn't really rocket science, just a practical, biblical way to pray the Word of God over yourself or the people you love. It's also the method we use in Million Praying Moms' Everyday Prayers journal library. Let me walk you through it step by step.

THINK

On each daily page, we give you a verse to pray to make it easy for you to follow this prayer method. However, you can always search the Scriptures for yourself to find a verse you'd like to pray instead. After you've chosen it, reflect on, process, and meditate over your verse. If you have time, read a few verses that come before and after your verse, or even the entire chapter of the Bible so you can have the proper context from which to understand it. Consider what God is speaking to your heart through His Word and through this verse. Dream about the future and what it might look like to see the message of this verse come to fruition in your life, or in your children's lives. In a small way, analyze the verse and figure out what you're inspired to pray.

PRAY

For almost ten years, my desire has been to allow my prayers to be inspired by God's Word. I try very hard not to take verses out of context, or use them for a purpose or meaning other than that which God intended for them. Reading the verse in context, as I just suggested, really helps with this. Once I've selected a verse, I craft it into a prayer. I usually stay as word-for-word as I can and then pray that verse back to God. You can see an example of a "Verse of the Day" and the prayer we craft from it for you on the daily pages of this journal.

Once you have your verse and prayer, use your thoughts about them as a jumping-off point to allow God's Word to move you and shape your prayers.

PRAISE

Praise is my favorite part of this method of prayer! Praising God is like putting on a pair of rose-colored glasses; it literally changes the way you see the world around you.

When we pause to deliberately reflect on the good things God is doing in our lives right now, it changes everything. (This can be even the tiniest of things we have to look hard to see, like having to clean for a Bible study group in your home. You might not want to clean, but at least you have people coming over to discuss the Word of God with you!) Instead of focusing on all we don't have or don't like (such as cleaning), gratitude for what we do have (being with brothers and sisters in Christ) blossoms in our hearts, truly making us joyful. Each day, I try to write down just a few things I'm grateful for, praising God for His continuous work of grace in my life.

BONUS

You might notice the lines for a to-do list on the daily pages. I love that little block because I find that when I sit down to pray, my mind gets flooded by all the things I need to do that day. Every. Single. Time. I feel the urgency of my schedule begin to take over, distracting me from the time I so desperately need in God's Word and prayer. Taking a minute to jot down my to-do list before I get started is kind of like doing a brain dump each day. If my list is written down, I won't forget what I have to do that day. This frees me up to spend the time I've allocated in prayer without worry stealing it from me.

PRAYER REQUESTS

Part of being a woman of prayer is interceding on behalf of others. My life literally changed the day a good friend held my hands in hers and said, "Let's pray about this now," instead of telling me, "I'll pray for you." You won't always be able to pray for others in person, but keeping track of their needs on a prayer list like the one at the bottom left of the daily pages is a great way to make sure you're being faithful to cover them in prayer.

GO!

I am so excited about the journey of prayer you hold in your hands. Each day begins with a devotion written specifically for you, and concludes with extra verses and questions for reflection that are a perfect way to take your study of patience to the next level or use with a group. We now consider you part of our Million Praying Moms family!

Connect with us at www.millionprayingmoms.com and keep us posted about the things God is doing in your life as you pray.

PART ONE

WHAT IS BIBLICAL PATIENCE?

Day 1

PATIENCE IS GETTING TO KNOW JESUS

But grow in the grace and knowledge of our Lord and Savior Jesus Christ. To him be the glory both now and to the day of eternity.　　　　　　　　　　　　　—2 Peter 3:18

I gave birth to my first son when I was twenty-seven years old. My second son, who came along just twenty-three months later, was born when I was twenty-nine. I remember my sister-in-law, who has known me since I was a little girl and is about ten years older, saying, "Brooke, I can't even believe you're old enough to have a baby." But I was. My husband and I had been married for just over two years when we found out we were expecting and gave birth just before our third anniversary. I had completed college and graduate school. I had even taken a few classes toward a Ph.D. (That program got dropped because said baby made mama so sick she couldn't finish her coursework.) I was working full time in pregnancy care ministry, and together, we made an okay living...certainly enough with the support of friends and family. On paper, I was ready to have children.

My maturity as a Christian is a slightly different story. To be clear, I made a decision to follow Jesus when I was just nine years old, and I chose to start walking very closely with Him when I was twenty-one. By the time my sons came along, I had developed and matured significantly as a believer, but I had a huge gap when it came to the spiritual skillset needed to fend off the lies the enemy threw at me when motherhood was much harder than I expected.

No, parenting did not come easily for me. Honestly, it still doesn't. I was a compliant child, one who liked to please her parents. I disciplined myself to get good grades without being told. Don't get me wrong, I wasn't an angel. I'm sure if you asked my mom, in particular, she could tell you some stories about my general mouthiness, laziness, or disobedience. But overall, I was a pretty good kid.

God, however, did not give me *compliant kids*. Both of my boys are good boys, and they love their family, but neither one of them is what I would call compliant. When they were little, they were downright difficult.

SOMETHING TO THINK ABOUT

In my book *Unraveled*, I described my experience during my children's early years this way:

> My boys often made me feel worn out, weary, and little bit like a failure sometimes, and my inner voice, the one that likes to show up and show me all my ugly, had a field day telling me I would never measure up as a mom.[1]

More often than not, I went to bed in those days feeling like I hadn't been the kind of mom I wanted to be. Admittedly, I didn't know much about being a mother to start with, but I did know one piece of information that would serve me well and help grow me into the mom I wanted to be: if I had any hope of bridging the gap, it would be accomplished by getting to know Jesus better. The answers to all my questions came through Him.

+ How do I survive the insane amount of noise in my home when I'm a raging introvert? Get to know Jesus better and allow Him to change me from the inside out.

+ How do I teach my children to respect me and respect the people they interact with?

+ Get to know Jesus better and allow Him to change me from the inside out.

---

1. Stacey Thacker and Brooke McGlothlin, *Unraveled: Hope for the Mom at the End of Her Rope* (Eugene, OR: Harvest House Publishers, 2022), 15.

- How do I help my children get along?
- Get to know Jesus better and allow Him to change me from the inside out.
- How can I show my children compassion when they mess up instead of getting mad at them?
- Get to know Jesus better and allow Him to change me from the inside out.
- How can I learn to set aside my own needs, so that I can more effectively meet theirs?
- Get to know Jesus better and allow Him to change me from the inside out.
- How can I make one more meal, wash one more load of laundry, or clean the floor one more time?
- Get to know Jesus better and allow Him to change me from the inside out.

I'm not trying to say that you can open your Bible and find the exact formula for controlling the noise in your home or a recipe for dinner when you are completely out of ideas. What I am saying is that the patience you need to survive and thrive in the moments of motherhood comes from your desire to *"grow in the grace and knowledge of our Lord and Savior Jesus Christ"* (2 Peter 3:18). Start there. Seriously, don't go anywhere else to get what you need. Just grow in your relationship with Jesus. It'll be enough.

EXTRA VERSES FOR STUDY OR PRAYER

Second Peter 1:3, 1:8

VERSE OF THE DAY

But grow in the grace and knowledge of our Lord and Savior Jesus Christ. To him be the glory both now and to the day of eternity.   —2 Peter 3:18

PRAYER

Father, I confess that I wish You had left us a roadmap for raising godly children. Sometimes I wish You'd audibly tell me how to have what I need for them every day, especially on the hard days when I feel like my patience has run right out. I feel like I need so much more than I have, but ultimately, what I need—who I need—is You. More of You. Give me the desire to know You more and grow me in grace. In Jesus's name, amen.

THINK

PRAY

PRAISE

TO-DO

PRAYER LIST

QUESTIONS FOR DEEPER REFLECTION

1. Do you really believe that Jesus has all the answers you need? If so, when did you make that decision? Do you remember when it happened?

2. If you aren't convinced Jesus holds all the answers, take some time to figure it out. Settle the answer today, before you move on. It's one of the most important decisions you'll ever make.

Day 2

PATIENCE IS KNOWING THE COST OF SALVATION

But I received mercy for this reason, so that in me, the worst of them, Christ Jesus might demonstrate his extraordinary patience as an example to those who would believe in him for eternal life.

—1 Timothy 1:16

When I was twenty-two years old, I took my first full-time job in ministry. I don't remember my exact job title, but I was basically the coordinator of counseling services at a local crisis pregnancy center in Staunton, Virginia. I split my time between encouraging, praying for, and training the lay counselors who served women in crisis pregnancy there and at the satellite office in Waynesboro.

The part of my job I loved the most was praying with the volunteers before their shift started. I can't tell you how much I learned about prayer during those times, both in praying for the women who were on the front lines of service and receiving their prayers as they covered me in the year leading up to my marriage. During that first year of full-time work, while I was finishing up my graduate studies, I realized the importance of spending daily time with the Lord in His Word and prayer. It only took working a few months, pouring out over and over again, to realize that I absolutely had to make time to pour God's Word back in. Thus began a lifelong habit of seeking God in prayer and time in the Bible each morning.

One particular morning, before I made my way to work, I found myself in 1 Timothy. Just a few short years before, I had read through the entire New Testament as a part of an elective class at Virginia Tech to finish up my degree. Since then, I'd been making my way back through the individual books of the New Testament. I remembered that I had fallen in love with Paul's letters to Timothy. I was a young minister myself at that time, and I felt a kinship with Timothy, who was so young as he attempted to follow God's plan for his life. I opened the pages of my Bible, casually read the beginning verses from Paul's first letter to his young friend…and stopped cold when I got to verses 12–17 of chapter one:

> I give thanks to Christ Jesus our Lord who has strengthened me, because he considered me faithful, appointing me to the ministry—even though I was formerly a blasphemer, a persecutor, and an arrogant man. But I received mercy because I acted out of ignorance in unbelief, and the grace of our Lord overflowed, along with the faith and love that are in Christ Jesus. This saying is trustworthy and deserving of full acceptance: "Christ Jesus came into the world to save sinners"—and I am the worst of them. But I received mercy for this reason, so that in me, the worst of them, Christ Jesus might demonstrate his extraordinary patience as an example to those who would believe in him for eternal life. Now to the King eternal, immortal, invisible, the only God, be honor and glory forever and ever. Amen.

SOMETHING TO THINK ABOUT

Have you ever had a moment in God's Word where you felt like the message was just for you? That's how I felt when I read Paul's words that morning. Quickly, the sins of my past came to mind, and I had a fresh realization of just how much it cost God to forgive me, just how much He had to forgive me for. Truly, I'm one of the worst of sinners. Friend, you are, too. We are all desperately in need of a Savior, even on our best days. Remembering this truth will serve us well and keep us in a position of praise to the God who saved us.

But look with me specifically at verse 16. Why did God save Paul? Why did He save you and me? *"So that in me, the worst of them,*

Christ Jesus might demonstrate his extraordinary patience as an example to those who would believe in him for eternal life."

As a mom, you serve as the biggest example to your children. Your life influences them the most. God saved you, at least in part, so that your life can serve to demonstrate His extraordinary patience as an example to them.

That's the real reason you can offer them patience in return.

God is doing exactly the same work in your children that He did in you, although in different ways, and it's all designed to bring them to Him. Your life is the biggest and best testimony of His grace they'll see for the first eighteen to twenty years of their lives. One day, God willing, they'll look back on all of the good, bad, and ugly of their own stories and see God's redeeming grace in just the same way.

EXTRA VERSES FOR STUDY OR PRAYER

Romans 2:4; Ephesians 2:7

VERSE OF THE DAY

But I received mercy for this reason, so that in me, the worst of them, Christ Jesus might demonstrate his extraordinary patience as an example to those who would believe in him for eternal life.

—1 Timothy 1:16

PRAYER

Father, thank You for the work You've done in my life. Thank You for saving me, for redeeming me, for changing me, and for setting my feet on a firm foundation. I praise You for demonstrating such extraordinary patience with me. Today, help me extend that patience to the people I love most. In Jesus's name, amen.

THINK

PRAY

PRAISE

TO-DO

PRAYER LIST

QUESTIONS FOR DEEPER REFLECTION

1. How long has it been since you paused to think about just how much Jesus saved you from? If it's been a while, re-read our verses in 1 Timothy and then allow your heart to be overwhelmed with gratitude.

2. Does thinking about all your Savior has done for you and all of the ways He has been patient with you over the years help you find a way to offer patience to those around you?

Day 3

PATIENCE IS A WORK OF CHARACTER

Rejoice in hope; be patient in affliction; be persistent in prayer.
—Romans 12:12

When my nephew was probably about six years old, he said something about his younger cousin, my niece, that turned into of those epic family sayings that last a lifetime. I'm not sure exactly what had happened in the moment to make him say it, but the fact that she was just shy of two years old made it even more hysterical.

He proclaimed, "She's a terrible distraction."

Aren't all two-year-olds a *terrible distraction?* I mean, I just can't think of a better description for a little one that age, but to hear another child just a few years older use that description was just icing on the cake. Now, many years later, my husband and I find ourselves using that descriptive phrase about all kinds of people and circumstances to add a bit of humor when things get hard.

In all seriousness, children can be terrible distractions. Distractions from the things we found meaning in before, distractions from important relationships, from the work we were doing for God's kingdom before they were born, even from our ability to get basic tasks done. I remember hearing one mom complain at a Bible study that her husband came home to a messy house and asked, "What have you been doing all day?" The truth was that she'd spent the day chasing her toddlers, keeping them alive, reading to them, making their lunches, rocking them to sleep for naptime, and then playing with them in the back yard until he got home, all while switching loads of laundry. Being a mom is a full-time job, with no pay and little thanks. Even now that my boys are older teenagers, I still find it hard to work as much when they're home. They're a distraction. And while they're distractions I dearly love, they still make it hard to get things done. This is why women sometimes feel that motherhood steals a part of who they are or makes them see a stranger looking back at them in the mirror.

I'm here to tell you that motherhood, when received through the lens of Romans 12:12, adds a fullness to our lives that doesn't come the same way through any other experience. There is a point to the hard things we encounter in motherhood, and that point can help us have the patience we need to endure them.

SOMETHING TO THINK ABOUT

If the definition of tribulation is "a cause of great trouble or suffering," then children are most definitely a kind of tribulation. I don't mean to devalue the beauty of motherhood at all. Nor do I want to take what is quite possibly the greatest source of joy in my life, apart from Jesus, and make it seem worse or harder than it really is. But children are hard, and there would be no need for hope without hardship. Neither would we persist in prayer if we didn't feel desperate for God to get us through tough times.

The theologian R. C. Sproul wrote, "Tribulation is inseparably related to hope, because when we are forced to suffer, the Holy Spirit uses those tribulations to work character in us and to provoke in our souls the virtue of hope."[2] Motherhood is almost directly responsible for the deepening of my personal prayer life because it caused tribulation. When I became a mother, I needed great amounts of hope, and my need for hope drove me to my knees in prayer directly to the One I knew could provide it. And that process, over time, gave me the very best gift possible—more of God Himself.

---

2. R. C. Sproul, *Romans: An Expositional Commentary* (Wheaton, IL: Crossway Books, 2019), 424.

He's worth it.

EXTRA VERSES FOR STUDY OR PRAYER

Acts 1:14; Hebrews 10:36

VERSE OF THE DAY

Rejoice in hope; be patient in affliction; be persistent in prayer.
—Romans 12:12

PRAYER

Father, I need hope. I need to remember that when tribulations come, there's a reason for them. Help me to remember that You are the source of my hope and turn to You in prayer as often as I need to so that I can have the patience I need to endure. In Jesus's name, amen.

THINK

PRAY

PRAISE

TO-DO

_____

_____

_____

PRAYER LIST

_____

_____

_____

QUESTIONS FOR DEEPER REFLECTION

1. Stop and take an evaluation of your prayer life. How often do you cry out to God or just invite Him into the moments of your day? Be honest, especially if it's less often than you'd care to admit.

    _____

    _____

2. Because of Jesus, believers have a direct line to God in the form of prayer. A _direct_ line. He's right there, friend, waiting for you to talk to Him, to ask Him for help. Even in the small decisions you think you ought to be able to make on your own, He's ready and willing to help. Will you ask?

    _____

    _____

Day 4

PATIENCE IS A FRUIT

But the fruit of the Spirit is love, joy, peace, patience, kindness, goodness, faithfulness, gentleness, and self-control. The law is not against such things. —Galatians 5:22–23

Recently, I taught a Sunday school class on the topic of peace. At the time, there was a lot of drama happening in our small community, and I personally had struggled with some anxiety related to my children. It was my opinion that a reminder about the source of our peace could serve us all well in that season. I truly, absolutely believe that God's Word has all of the answers to every problem, so I walked the class through a step-by-step process for overcoming anxiety that came straight from the Bible. More than that, it's the process I use in my own daily life, in the midst of various forms of stress and worry, to get back to a place of peace and trust in God. That process is outlined in *Everyday Prayers for Peace*,[3] another prayer journal in this series.

Ironically—or perhaps not—God put my teaching to the test just two days later at a junior varsity football game, of all places…and my kid wasn't even playing! The game was a little more lopsided than I'd hoped for, so my mind started to drift to the upcoming baseball tournament both of my children would be playing in the next weekend. I confess that while I love baseball and all the life lessons it has taught my children and me about life, it is also a source of great stress. Over the last summer, I experienced several symptoms directed related to anxiety every time my children stepped up to bat, including an elevated

---

3. Brooke McGlothlin, *Everyday Prayers for Peace: A 30-Day Devotional & Reflective Journal for Women* (New Kensington, PA: Whitaker House, 2022).

heart rate that easily approached 140 beats per minute. This led me to keep saying *panic prayers* that only seemed to make me feel worse.

Now, any good baseball mom—or any other kind of sports mom for that matter—knows that she has very little control over what happens when her child is at bat or in the thick of the game. Preparation leading up to that point, both physical and mental, is what impacts that moment the most. I've learned to be outwardly quiet except for an initial, "Let's go!" as I yell out my sons' jersey numbers. But over the summer, my insides were anything but quiet. In fact, they were a roiling, boiling mess. The intensity of my prayers, while well-intentioned, didn't match the situation at hand. I prayed for my sons to have a good at bat with as much emotion as if I were praying for them to live after an accident. I knew it, but I had a hard time stopping it until God reminded me of this truth:

Peace is not a feeling; it's a fruit.

SOMETHING TO THINK ABOUT

According to our Scripture passage today, peace—and all of the other eight traits that characterize the life of a believer in Jesus—is something God's Spirit plants in our hearts at our salvation, and then grows into maturity as we pursue knowing Him more and more.

I don't want you to miss this: if you have a relationship with Jesus, you already have a seed of love, joy, peace, patience, kindness, goodness, faithfulness, gentleness, and self-control planted in your heart. Yes, I've been talking about peace today, but don't forget that patience is on the list too.

You may not feel like you have a lot of patience to offer your children, but remember that patience is fruit, not a feeling. There is some measure of patience already lurking in your redeemed heart, and with God's help, it can grow into something beautiful that helps you live your life in a way that brings glory to God and makes others wonder what you have that they need.

Press in. Feed your fruit. Watch it grow.

EXTRA VERSES FOR STUDY OR PRAYER

Colossians 3:13; 1 Peter 3:8

VERSE OF THE DAY

But the fruit of the Spirit is love, joy, peace, patience, kindness, goodness, faithfulness, gentleness, and self-control. The law is not against such things. —Galatians 5:22–23

PRAYER

Father, grow patience in me. While You're at it, grow love, joy, peace, kindness, goodness, faithfulness, gentleness, and self-control. Thank You for planting these seeds in my heart when You saved me. Grow them over time so that I look more and more like You. In Jesus's name, amen.

THINK

PRAY

PRAISE

TO-DO

PRAYER LIST

QUESTIONS FOR DEEPER REFLECTION

1. We all know our patience can be tried, but have you ever thought of patience as something you can invest in and grow?

2. In order for plants to grow, they need time, attention, water, sunlight, and good soil. How can you apply this concept to the growth of your patience?

Day 5

PATIENCE IS LOVING THROUGH THE HARD

With all humility and gentleness, with patience, bearing with one another in love.　　　　　　　　　　—Ephesians 4:2

A few weeks ago in church, our pastor had us look deeply at Colossians 3:1–17. During the evening service, we made a list of all the parts of our earthly nature we need to put off—such as impurity, lust, evil desires, greed, and more—and all of the parts of the new self we should put on if we're in Christ, like compassion, kindness, humility, and patience, just to name a few.

What stood out to me the most is that we are urged to *"put on compassion, kindness, humility, gentleness, and patience, bearing with one another"* (verses 12–13). I've found myself praying for a greater ability to bear with others since that evening.

According to my pastor, to *bear with one another* means understanding that we all have faults or blind spots, so we must make space for those things in our relationships. Expecting others to be just like us or to never get on our nerves is unrealistic. I have habits that drive other people crazy. You do, too. They're part of what makes us unique, but they can make relationships hard. In this verse, Paul is telling us to have patience with one another and to offer gentleness and humility (considering someone else more important than ourselves) in the face of those difficult things.

This extends to the relationships we have with our children, too. Both of my sons are noisy, which can be unbearable at times for introverted me. They aren't *trying* to get on my nerves when they are whistling in the car or beat-boxing in the hallway. They're just being their own happy selves. It's up to me to offer them patient correction when needed, allow them to be who they are when I can, and teach them to respect others around them at the same time.

Bearing with one another even pertains to the sibling relationships in our lives and in our homes. I've often said that no one, *no one*, knows how to get under my skin as quickly as my big brother does. Don't get me wrong, I love him, and I would do almost anything for him, but he knows how to push my buttons, and he often does. I'm 100 percent sure I do the same for him. We have the same parents and were raised in the same house, but we couldn't be more different. My children are the same way. Born twenty-three months apart, they are *poles apart*. Sometimes I don't even think they look or act like siblings.

SOMETHING TO THINK ABOUT

During the pandemic, at least during the first few weeks, I thought my sons' relationship might spontaneously combust. They drove each other—and me—crazy to the point that I began to pray specifically for the Lord to help their relationship. We had long talks about the way they were treating each other and supporting each other. We looked at key passages from the Bible that define not just how to treat a brother in Christ but how to treat a biological brother who happens to be a Christian. The changes were slow in coming, even though they literally had nothing else to do but be together. None of their friends could come over, so out of necessity, my gasoline and fire boys spent time hanging out. I saw them start to be creative together, playing outside on our property and talking to each other in ways they hadn't for a long time. It wasn't perfect and I had no expectation that it would be, but I believe God worked Ephesians 4:2 in their hearts...at least a little bit.

For my family, at least for the two siblings in my home, the pandemic was a good thing. It forced my sons to learn to be more patient with each other. Even though things have been back to normal for a while now, I still think it changed their relationship for the better, laying a foundation that, thankfully, outlasted the struggles of all that togetherness. For that, I am eternally grateful.

I've always said that if I could help my boys learn to get along with each other, they'd be able to get along with anyone. There will always be difficult people in their lives—teachers, coaches, bosses, coworkers, and friends. Learning to look for the good in others and bear with their faults is one of the most important skills our children can have.

Us too.

EXTRA VERSES FOR STUDY OR PRAYER

Colossians 3:16; 1 Peter 4:8

VERSE OF THE DAY

With all humility and gentleness, with patience, bearing with one another in love.   —Ephesians 4:2

PRAYER

Father, when I'm tempted to get irritated at someone for something that's just a part of who they are, help me to remember that I'm not perfect myself, so that I can offer them grace and patience. In Jesus's name, amen.

THINK

_____

_____

PRAY

_____

_____

PRAISE

TO-DO

PRAYER LIST

QUESTIONS FOR DEEPER REFLECTION

1. Is there someone in your life who just drives you crazy? Someone you find it difficult to be around? Write down some ways you can bear with them, like Jesus bears with you.

2. Humility means to consider someone more important than yourself. How does this definition affect your ability to extend grace to a difficult person in your life?

Day 6

PATIENCE IS CONFIDENCE IN WHAT WE CAN'T SEE

Let us not get tired of doing good, for we will reap at the proper time if we don't give up. —Galatians 6:9

A friend of mine recently posted these words on her Facebook account:

Being different is hard.

Choosing a different path is hard.

Trying to not care about the temporary is hard.

And. Being a parent is hard. Feeling like you are responsible for their happiness and success is a weight we aren't really meant to carry, but we do. I know God's writing a story for all of them that I can't screw up...but some days, it does feel really heavy, and I wish I could just rest in the truth of what I know.

I replied to her post with these words:

I prayed for God to give me boys, so I could raise men who are different (I thought it was more about me back then and forgot God is in charge). For some reason, it took me years to realize that raising boys to be different would, in fact, make them different and that being different might be really hard for them. Worth it? Yes. Heavy? Yes.

It's hard for our kids to look at what's happening around them and not get frustrated. For that matter, it's hard for adults. I have often prayed, "Lord, why does it seem like the harder we try to do what's right, the more it costs us? Why do my right decisions affect my children negatively? Shouldn't we be rewarded in some way?"

I'm forty-five, and sometimes, I get tired of doing good. And if I find this concept hard to understand, it's no wonder my teenagers struggle with it from time to time. They wonder, I know, if staying on the right path is really worth it.

There are so many temptations, distractions, and detours our children can take in this life. I used to spend all of my time praying for my children to come to salvation through faith in Jesus. Now that they have, most days I just pray for God to keep them. I don't mean keep their salvation—personally, I don't believe that can be lost—but what I mean is that I want God to keep them on the right path, keep their eyes on Him, keep their hearts from evil, and keep them strong when they're faced with temptation. Sometimes, when they stop and take stock of the world around them, it feels like evil is winning, and that's hard. They get tired of doing good and choosing the right thing when it feels like choosing the wrong thing would be so much easier, perhaps even more fun.

SOMETHING TO THINK ABOUT

The definition of faith is complete trust or confidence in someone or something. As the Bible tells us, *"Now faith is the reality of what is hoped for, the proof of what is not seen"* (Hebrews 11:1). This is especially true for us as Christians. We ask our children to choose what's right, sacrificing their reputation, enduring bullying, and sometimes being left out or worse—and for what in return? A reward they can't see, touch, taste, or feel? That's the question. What do we actually get in return for not growing tired of doing good?

The answer is that we get the favor of God. More of God. The riches of a deep, clean, pure relationship with the Father, and those things are more important than the favor of man. You and I know that because we're more mature in Christ than our children are. We see the benefits of walking with the Lord, even in our weak moments, and staying on the right paths because, more than likely, we've experienced it the other way around. Having made some wrong turns and taken some wrong paths ourselves, we want to spare our children from enduring the same. So we do our best, knowing that asking them to be different will cost them at times and maybe cost them a lot.

Is it worth it? Yes. Is it heavy? Yes. So I keep praying that God will show my children the value of being people of worth, people who follow hard after God, and, in the end, people who will not grow tired from doing good.

Lord, keep them.

EXTRA VERSES FOR STUDY OR PRAYER
Isaiah 40:31; 1 Corinthians 15:58

VERSE OF THE DAY

Let us not get tired of doing good, for we will reap at the proper time if we don't give up. —Galatians 6:9

PRAYER

Father, please keep my children. Give them more of You inside of each struggle they face. Each time they feel different for trying to follow You, give them courage to do what's right. In Jesus's name, amen.

THINK

PRAY

PRAISE

TO-DO   *PRAYER LIST*

QUESTIONS FOR DEEPER REFLECTION

1. Do your children ever get ridiculed for being different from other people because they're part of a Christian family? How do you help them through it?

2. How do you deal with your own feelings about raising kids who are different?

Day 7

PATIENCE IS LOSING CONTROL

Patience is better than power, and controlling one's emotions, than capturing a city.   —Proverbs 16:32

Losing control of our emotions, at its heart, is about a lack of power.

I know that seems like a bold statement to start a devotion, but I wanted to get right to the point. Before I had children, I didn't realize I had a problem controlling my emotions. I knew I liked being in control, but my situations pre-children never caused me to lose control of myself. I look back now, with the perspective of almost twenty years, and I can see hints here and there, but I really didn't know I had something sinister lurking in my heart until the right set of circumstances made it spill out. And that set of circumstances were my two boys.

Maybe it was because my husband has always worked shift work and never ever had a normal schedule. Maybe it was because God gave me two of *those* boys—the ones who are 250 percent boy, loud, aggressive, impulsive, and...did I say loud? Or maybe it was just because I am not naturally gifted with younger children. Whatever the reason, my children brought out the worst in me more than I'd care to remember. They showed me that a monster lived in my heart, a monster that looked much like a mad two-year-old who hadn't gotten her way. I stamped my feet (figuratively and perhaps literally) a few times as a young mother because I couldn't get my children to act the way I wanted them to.

I lost control, lost my patience, and lost my emotions.

Patience is required for military conquests, those of old and those today. I don't think we need to see our children as military adversaries, but they will often feel like the opposition. And while there may not be many parenting formulas given in the Bible, there is certainly a theme of strategic action in both the Old and New Testaments that encourages us to control what comes out of our hearts and mouths so that we can have a kingdom impact on those around us. According to today's verse, this is harder to do than overtaking an entire city, but there is a way.

SOMETHING TO THINK ABOUT

I find it interesting that Paul's warning to *"put on the full armor of God"* (Ephesians 6:11) comes just a few verses after he talks about the relationship between parents and their children. It's almost like he knew there would be struggle here and gave us the tools we need to be patient and be careful what we say. I love that he uses wartime language because learning to control ourselves is letting go of our need for power and doing battle in God's power instead:

> *Take up the full armor of God, so that you may be able to resist in the evil day, and having prepared everything, to take your stand. Stand, therefore, with truth like a belt around your waist, righteousness like armor on your chest, and your feet sandaled with readiness for the gospel of peace. In every situation take up the shield of faith with which you can extinguish all the flaming arrows of the evil one. Take the helmet of salvation and the sword of the Spirit—which is the word of God. Pray at all times in the Spirit with every prayer and request, and stay alert with all perseverance and intercession for all the saints.* (Ephesians 6:13–18)

What does a mom need to wear each day in order to find true power and have patience with her children?

+ The belt of truth: time in God's Word. Only the truth can push out the lies of the world.

- The armor of righteousness: knowing Who you belong to at all times and making sure your identity is firmly rooted in this.

- The sandals of the gospel: preparing you for walking into situations where you can be the peace that comes from knowing Jesus.

- The shield of faith: against the roller coaster of life, the unknowns, and the plans of the enemy.

- The helmet of salvation: to cover your most important asset, your mind, with the knowledge of your salvation, empowered by your knowledge and faith in the Word of God.

- And prayer: at all times and in every way.

Put on the whole armor and invite God into your mess. Let it be His power that conquers your home and gives you peace.

EXTRA VERSES FOR STUDY OR PRAYER

Proverbs 14:29; James 1:19

VERSE OF THE DAY

Patience is better than power, and controlling one's emotions, than capturing a city.   —Proverbs 16:32

PRAYER

Father, help me to make good use of the tools You've made available to me in Your Word—those that can change me from the inside out and prepare me for battle—so that I can be all You desire me to be for those I love most. In Jesus's name, amen.

THINK

PRAY

_____

_____

PRAISE

_____

_____

TO-DO

_____

_____

_____

PRAYER LIST

_____

_____

_____

QUESTIONS FOR DEEPER REFLECTION

1. Do you ever feel like you and your children are on different teams? Like you're fighting against them more than you fight for them?

2. Try putting on the armor of God every morning for the next thirty days. Write out each step and literally talk to God, telling Him what you're doing aloud. For example, "Lord, I'm putting on the belt of truth. Help the truth of Your Word drown out the lies of the world today." Bring this passage to the forefront of your mind and make it come into the moments of your day. Then write a journal entry about what God did.

Day 8

PATIENCE IS WAITING WITH EXPECTATION

Be silent before the LORD and wait expectantly for him; do not be agitated by one who prospers in his way, by the person who carries out evil plans. —Psalm 37:7

It is so hard to be silent before the Lord and wait on Him to act. Can we just get that off of our chests and admit it right from the start? To make it even harder, this verse says we should wait patiently, like we believe with all of our hearts that God is about to move. I don't know about you, but I think I'm more likely to wait impatiently—grumbling, complaining, and struggling to believe God is going to come through somehow.

In my heart, I long to be the kind of woman who is full of faith in the God who *can*. I want to be someone whose overflow is trust, faith, and joy, but the truth is that I have to work for those things. Maybe you do, too?

I think it's the more common human experience. In fact, I think long life—maturing and growing in our faith as we face adversity and challenge—is the classroom where faith, trust, and joy are learned.

My oldest son loves baseball, and it's been his dream to play college baseball since around age eleven. One week to the day after he received an offer to play for our local community college, he got hurt in a baseball event. He was throwing from shortstop to first base when the ligament in his throwing arm pulled bone from bone, fracturing his elbow. One week after we were weeping with joy over the fulfillment of his dream, we found ourselves weeping with questions, wondering if he would ever play baseball again.

The only question that ran through our minds as we tried to process the whiplash-like circumstances of the last week, was "Why, Lord? He's been through so much already. He's a good boy. He loves You. He has worked so hard to get here and overcome so much. Why, Lord? Why?"

I'm a talker. I almost always have something to say, some form of encouragement I can give to my children even if I don't have the exact answer they need. But that night, after we got home from urgent care with his arm bound in a temporary cast and his dreams in a puddle at his feet, I had no words. My husband had no words. Even my younger son, who is known for being full of words, stayed quiet. We were silent before the Lord not because we wanted to be, but because we couldn't be anything else.

And then God stepped in.

SOMETHING TO THINK ABOUT

An hour or so after we got home from urgent care, my husband got a phone call from our pastor. He had seen my prayer request text to our Sunday school class when Sunday evening service was over and knew he had to come to us. Our pastor is also our friend, and he knows how important and how deeply meaningful this baseball journey had been.

When our pastor showed up at our door, he came in, gently put his hands on our son's shoulders, and said, "This is a defining moment, but it does not define you. You are more than baseball. If the Lord uses this to redirect you, you needed to be redirected. If He doesn't, He'll show you another way, and the process of it will make you a stronger man. God can handle all your emotions, so be honest with Him, but don't turn away from Him. If this has to define your road ahead, let it be toward Him."

He then prayed with us and went home.

The next morning, I woke up with Romans 8:28 on my heart: "*We know that all things work together for the good of those who love God, who are called according to his purpose.*" I remembered writing the story of our son's baseball journey in my prayer journal. God kept reminding me that the verse says, "all things," meaning God works everything—the great, the good, the bad, and the horrible, even the mundane—together for good, for those who are called according to His purpose. This potentially devastating injury? It would be used for good, too, and we had to trust in that.

At school, one of our son's favorite coaches called him into his office. He looked at my son, with his big, bulky makeshift cast on, and said, "I know you think this is the worst, the absolute worst, thing that could ever happen, but I don't believe God would've given you this if it didn't have a purpose for you. You can handle this, and we're with you."

Man, what a show of support. Not just from pastors and favorite coaches, but from God Himself. Our family was blown away that God would choose to use all of these people to surround our son with that kind of strong, steady encouragement right when he needed it most, and when, for some reason, we had no words ourselves. As we were silent and waited for God to show up, God made a way to reach our son's heart. That is the beautiful picture of how God uses all things for good; we just have to wait on Him to do it. He isn't bound by our dreams, our timetable, or even our very best words, but He is bound by His Word. We can trust it, even expectantly wait for it, because He will do what He says He will do.

EXTRA VERSES FOR STUDY OR PRAYER

Psalm 40:1; Psalm 62:5

VERSE OF THE DAY

Be silent before the Lord and wait expectantly for him; do not be agitated by one who prospers in his way, by the person who carries out evil plans.   —Psalm 37:7

PRAYER

Father, I know it takes time to build trust. Please (gently) build that trust in me, so that I can be silent and wait expectantly for You to move, both for me and for those I love. In Jesus's name, amen.

THINK

PRAY

PRAISE

TO-DO

PRAYER LIST

QUESTIONS FOR DEEPER REFLECTION

1. Have you ever watched your child get hurt or potentially lose something of great importance to them? How did you handle it?

2.   Make a list of all the ways God has provided for your family over the years. I'm not talking just about financial provisions, but also opportunities, redeeming moments, or healing. Stick that list in your Bible, and when you're tempted to lose hope that God will act on your behalf, pull it out as a reminder of His goodness.

Day 9

PATIENCE IS RECOGNIZING GOD'S VOICE

Wait for the LORD; *be strong, and let your heart be courageous.*
Wait for the LORD. —Psalm 27:14

When I was sixteen years old, I took a trip from the mountains of southwestern Virginia to Birmingham, Alabama. I was a part of Acteens, a missions-minded group for young teenage girls. Part of the training and preparation for our local group's home missions trip was to attend the National Acteens Convention. It was there that I saw Point of Grace in concert for the first time. All of the girls on the trip fell in love with them. They were brand new to the Christian music scene, and their music gave us a legitimate, truth-filled alternative to what we were used to hearing on the radio. Our leaders bought each of us a tape of their music to take home (yes, I know I'm dating myself). We all loved those tapes, but I don't think my leaders knew just how much that one act of kindness would shape my life.

Where I grew up, in the mountains, we didn't have a Christian radio station. Most often, I listened to the Top 40s or country music; in church, we sang from the Baptist hymnal. I also loved bluegrass and old-time music (and still do), but I didn't even really know contemporary Christian music existed until that concert in Alabama. I became absolutely hooked on Point of Grace's music and message, so I have attended many of their concerts over the years. I've read all of their books, and God used them to keep me on the right path in so many ways. At times, their hope-filled, gospel-saturated message was the only thing that kept me tethered to the God I wanted to serve.

One of their albums in particular, titled *Steady On*, became the anthem of my college years. I remember listening often to the title track and being struck by these lyrics:

> We run up ahead, we lag behind you
> It's hard to wait when heaven's on our mind
> Teach our restless feet to walk beside you
> 'Cause in our hearts we're already gone
> Will you walk with us
> Steady on[4]

In that season, I was trying to figure out what I wanted to do with my life. My original plan had been to go straight from college to seminary. With a forthcoming degree in psychology, I found myself wanting to know more about what God's Word had to say about the human heart and mind, so it seemed logical that seminary was the place to go next. I remember praying, "Lord, show me the right path. Show me where to go. I want to walk beside You, not in front of or behind You. Help me hear Your voice and follow Your leading for today."

However, when my parents and I visited the seminary I had planned to attend, I didn't feel God's peace. I knew it wasn't where I was supposed to go, but I had no earthly idea what that meant or where I would end up.

A friend told me about Liberty University. You would think that having grown up in Virginia, I would've known about a Christian college practically in my backyard, but I didn't, and I had no idea they had a professional counseling program, the very field I wanted to study. On a whim, my then-boyfriend (now husband) and I hopped into his truck, drove to Lynchburg, and toured the campus. I knew the moment I put my feet on the ground there that it was the place for me. True enough, God used my time there to grow me in exponential ways.

I don't want to know what might've happened had I not waited on and listened to the Lord on where to finish my education. But how did I know what I was hearing was the Lord's voice?

4. Point of Grace, "Steady On," on *Steady On* (Word Records/Sony Records, 1998).

SOMETHING TO THINK ABOUT

According to recent statistics from Lifeway Research, only 27 percent of professing Christians read the Bible a few times a week.[5] Only 27 percent! This tells me that 73 percent of the people who say they know God don't know Him very well at all.

God reveals Himself to us through His Word.

God proves Himself to us through His Word.

God changes our hearts to look more like His through His Word.

And...God speaks to us through His Word.

That's how I know when God speaks to me. I recognize Him because I know what His voice sounds like. He speaks to me through His Word.

This doesn't mean hearing from God or listening to God will be foolproof. We should always measure what we think God is telling us against His Word and be willing to change our ideas if they don't measure up. But when we spend time getting to know God, our ability to do that increases over time.

Sometimes it's a still, small voice, a nudge in the right direction. Other times, God might use a mature wise counselor to get your attention or a sermon at church. It might just be a feeling you can't shake, like when I visited the seminary. Mostly, learning to listen to God's voice and know when He's speaking to you is a matter of experience.

In the beginning, take Him at His Word...literally. Read His Word and consider it His message to you personally. Do what it says. That is what listening to God looks like on a foundational level. Then, the more you live that way, the easier it will be to recognize the voice of your Savior speaking to you on a heart level. Psalm 119:11 says, *"I have treasured your word in my heart so that I may not sin against you."*

5. Aaron Earls, "More Americans Read the Bible During the Pandemic," Lifeway Research, October 21, 2021; research.lifeway.com/2021/10/21/more-americans-read-the-bible-during-the-pandemic.

Store up God's Word in your heart, so that when He speaks, you can recognize His voice.

Steady on.

EXTRA VERSES FOR STUDY OR PRAYER

Psalm 31:24; Psalm 37:34

VERSE OF THE DAY

Wait for the LORD*; be strong, and let your heart be courageous. Wait for the* LORD*.*   —Psalm 27:14

PRAYER

Father, I'm Your sheep. Help me to recognize Your voice and know when You're speaking to me so that I can only walk where You want me to walk, go where You want me to go, and lead my children where You want them. In Jesus's name, amen.

THINK

PRAY

PRAISE

TO-DO

PRAYER LIST

QUESTIONS FOR DEEPER REFLECTION

1. Have you ever had God change directions on you, leading you in a different way when you thought you already had a plan?

2. Reflect on a time when God spoke to your heart. What was it like? Write it down and begin to notice what happens when God talks to you.

Day 10

PATIENCE IS TRUSTING GOD WITH THE FIGHT

The LORD will fight for you; you need only to be still.
—Exodus 14:14 (NIV)

Imagine having to leave your home—the only place you'd ever known—quickly and without warning, in the middle of the night, knowing you'd probably never return. And imagine this happening after watching your entire community experience enough death and destruction to rip out its very soul.

The Israelites experienced this very thing when God told them to leave Egypt. After the tenth and final plague upon the Egyptians in which the Lord struck down all of the firstborns in the land, human and animal alike, Pharaoh finally let them go. Having lost his own firstborn, along with so many others who did not have the protection of the one true God, Pharaoh and all of Egypt groaned under the weight of the enormous loss. In that pain, he relented and let God's people go.

They had to escape fast, leaving behind much of their belongings. They had to trust in God's promise that He would lead them to *"a land flowing with milk and honey"* (Exodus 13:5). From there, God gave them instructions, telling them to share with their children what He had done for them as He led them on their journey with a pillar of cloud by day and a pillar of fire by night. The Scriptures say that God *"did not depart from before the people"* (Exodus 13:22 ESV).

For God's people, it must have seemed like a great victory—and it was. There they were being led out of Egypt right under Pharaoh's nose. I imagine many of them thought they would get to the promised land within just a few days and were filled with trust in the God whose mighty works they had just seen ten times in a row before leaving Egypt.

I've often wished God would give me a sign. It's always been hard for me to understand why the Israelites got so grumpy when God showed Himself to them in such miraculous ways. Who wouldn't be filled with faith at a pillar of cloud or a pillar of fire to lead the way? Little did they know that the same God was leading them and strategically positioning them for something greater, intentionally placing them in a spot where if He didn't show up, nothing happened.

In chapter 14, we read:

Then the Lord spoke to Moses: "Tell the Israelites to turn back and camp in front of Pi-hahiroth, between Migdol and the sea; you must camp in front of Baal-zephon, facing it by the sea. Pharaoh will say of the Israelites: They are wandering around the land in confusion; the wilderness has boxed them in. I will harden Pharaoh's heart so that he will pursue them. Then I will receive glory by means of Pharaoh and all his army, and the Egyptians will know that I am the Lord." So the Israelites did this. (Exodus 14:1–4)

I've known the story of the exodus and the parting of the Red Sea since I was a child in Sunday school. I've read how Pharaoh led his armies to recapture the Israelites and believed he had trapped them between his armies and the sea, with nowhere to go, no way of escape. I have gloried at the God who could part the Red Sea, allow His people to walk over a dry seabed, and then allow the waters to fall on the armies of the Egyptians, killing them all and saving His people when it looked like there was no salvation in sight. But for some reason, it never dawned on me that God told them to be right where they were when Pharaoh caught up to them.

It was His plan all along.

SOMETHING TO THINK ABOUT

The question I have to ask myself—and I'm sure you're asking it too—is why in the world God would intentionally move His people into danger? Why would a good God place His people in harm's way?

In my book *Gospel-Centered Mom,*[6] I explore the story of Hosea, an Old Testament prophet. The Lord asked Hosea to marry a prostitute, and their love story wasn't all roses and kittens. Throughout the course of their marriage, his wife Gomer was unfaithful to him, returning to her life of ruin instead of allowing herself to be loved. We're not even sure that the children their marriage produced belonged to Hosea. Yet, over and over, God instructed Hosea to go get her. I wrote:

> It's unthinkable, really, that God would ask a man like Hosea
> to endure such a thing. But…perhaps God created him to be
> a part of His story for a specific purpose—to display His
> power, love, grace, and plan of redemption to the onlook-
> ing world, and to us who are reading about it many years
> later. Maybe God didn't make Hosea, or us, so He could be
> a part of our story. Maybe it's supposed to be the other way
> around.[7]

God will fight for us, and He will strategically place us in situations in which we demonstrate His power and love to the onlooking world as we choose to be still in His purposeful will. I don't necessarily understand that, but it's clear from Scripture that He does this. We have always and only been created to bring glory to God. It's our most important purpose. The good news is that God is 100 percent committed to His glory. That's how we know we can always expect His goodness toward those of us who believe.

---

6. Brooke McGlothlin, *Gospel-Centered Mom: The Freeing Truth About What Your Kids Really Need* (New York: Multnomah, 2017), 53–54.
7. Ibid.

EXTRA VERSES FOR STUDY OR PRAYER

Exodus 14; Deuteronomy 3:22

VERSE OF THE DAY

The Lord will fight for you; you need only to be still.
                                                    —Exodus 14:14 NIV

PRAYER

Father, help me to be still in Your purposeful will, knowing that You have placed me and my family in this place so that You can demonstrate Your goodness to those around us. Please let our lives be a living testimony of Your power and love. In Jesus's name, amen.

THINK

_____

_____

PRAY

_____

_____

PRAISE

_____

_____

TO-DO   PRAYER LIST

_____   _____

_____   _____

_____   _____

QUESTIONS FOR DEEPER REFLECTION

1. Have you ever been through something difficult that seemed to have no purpose? According to today's devotion, what might the eternal purpose have been?

2. Think of a time when God fought for you. Write it down in your journal so you can remember what it felt like to know the God of the universe came to your rescue.

Day 11

PATIENCE IS MAKING ROOM FOR GOD

The Lord does not delay his promise, as some understand delay, but is patient with you, not wanting any to perish but all to come to repentance. —2 Peter 3:9

One of the main reasons I love to pray the Word of God and encourage and teach others to do the same is because I believe God will always be true to it. There may not be many specific instructions for parents in the Bible, but there are plenty of promises to God's children. One of those, in Isaiah 55:11, is that God's Word will not return void, but will do exactly what He purposes for it to do.

There's confidence in that promise...and a bit of mystery. On the one hand, we can have the assurance that when God's Word goes forth, it will accomplish His specific and purposeful plan. On the other hand, we have no control over what God's plan actually is. My main takeaway, in the almost twenty years I've been praying God's Word, is that I can have faith in God's powerful promise without having to understand its purpose or His timetable in fulfilling it.

I started this prayer journal with the words, "Give them the grace to grow out of this," and shared that it was something God impressed upon my heart as a gift I can give my children while they grow, mature, and learn more about Him. But I'm convinced that it's the same gift God offers to all of us as His children, even and especially as we grow up and age. Today's verse assures us that the Lord does not delay in fulfilling His promises. While the entire passage from 2 Peter 3 is speaking mainly about the day of the Lord, or when Jesus returns, I don't think it's wrong to apply it to other situations when we are waiting for the Lord to show up, or feeling like the Lord is silent or maybe even delayed.

Have you been praying for a child to come to Christ, with no direct answer in sight?

Do you have a prodigal child who has not looked back, despite your bleeding prayers?

Has sickness or injury entered your home and caused you to fall on your knees like never before?

Are you watching a child experience hurt while you are unable to kiss away the pain or offer assurance that it will be alright?

One of my favorite books on prayer, *If You Will Ask*, is a collection of sermons and writings on prayer by Oswald Chambers.[8] In that book, Chambers says, "God's silences are His answers. If we only take as answers those that are visible to our senses, we are in a very elementary condition of grace." Sometimes if *feels* like God is delayed. Sometimes it feels like He's being too quiet. However, this is only because we're trying to understand our circumstances the way we can, within our own limits, and failing to recognize that God's ways are altogether different from ours. God doesn't delay as we might understand it. He's just on an entirely different timetable that we can't see.

SOMETHING TO THINK ABOUT

The thing is, I want a visible answer. I can't help it. I bet you're mostly the same way, especially when it comes to our children. I really do want to wake up every morning full of faith that God will show up, trusting in His perfect timing because I know even His silences and His seeming delays are for my children's good. God is growing me into that woman, but it isn't yet the standard default of my heart. Too much of me still lives in the temporal and too easily forgets the eternal.

---

8. Oswald Chambers, *If You Will Ask: Reflections on the Power of Prayer* (Grand Rapids, MI: Our Daily Bread Publishing, 2012).

Could it be that a different perspective entirely exists than the one that makes me feel like God is holding out on me?

Chambers goes on to say, "Some prayers are followed by silence... because they are bigger than we can understand. Can God trust you like that? Remember that Jesus Christ's silences are always signs that He knows we can stand a bigger revelation than we think we can."[9] Maybe God isn't answering the way we want because there's something more for us to learn through the experience? What if instead of trying everything in our power to get out of what's hurting us, we just leaned in and listened, making room for God's plans, even if they aren't what we want?

EXTRA VERSES FOR STUDY OR PRAYER

Isaiah 30:18; Luke 18:2–8

VERSE OF THE DAY

The Lord does not delay his promise, as some understand delay, but is patient with you, not wanting any to perish but all to come to repentance.   —2 Peter 3:9

PRAYER

Father, thank You that I can trust Your timing. Help my family to trust it as well, especially when it feels like You're being too quiet or that Your response is delayed. Broaden our minds and hearts to make room for Your plans, even if they aren't what we want. In Jesus's name, amen.

THINK

_____

_____

---

9. Ibid.

PRAY

PRAISE

TO-DO   PRAYER LIST

QUESTIONS FOR DEEPER REFLECTION

1. Is God being silent in your life right now? Set aside your feelings about His silence for a moment and ask Him what He needs to show You about Himself in the midst of it.

2. Chambers says, "If we only take as answers those that are visible to our senses, we are in a very elementary condition of grace." This insinuates that those who require a sign or a visible answer of some kind are immature believers. I'll readily admit that, at times, and by this definition, I'm an immature believer. But I want to grow up in my faith. Do you?

Day 12

PATIENCE IS KNOWING WE NEED JESUS

And if he sins against you seven times in a day, and comes back to you seven times, saying, "I repent," you must forgive him. The apostles said to the Lord, "Increase our faith." —Luke 17:4–5

When my kids were very little and I caught them doing something they had been told not to, I would kneel down beside them and say, "You can't obey on your own. You need Jesus's help to do it. Ask Him to help you obey." I took this straight from Elyse Fitzpatrick's book *Give Them Grace: Dazzling Your Kids with the Love of Jesus*,[10] and it was a wonderful, gospel-centered way to help them understand that sin or willful disobedience is not something we can overcome on our own. Sin must be accounted for and forgiven, confessed and overcome. To do this, we need Jesus.

Thankfully, Jesus is more than ready to help. One night, after a long day of dealing with the same basic sin over and over again, I sent my son to his room for an early bedtime. We needed a break from each other, and I needed to be able to think straight and pray. I was tired of telling him that he needed Jesus that day, and I wanted him to repent. Truthfully, my desire had more to do with me than it did him. Telling our children they need Jesus requires first knowing we need Jesus…at least telling them in the right spirit…and I wasn't in the right spirit. Love required me to forgive him again and again

---

10. Elyse M. Fitzpatrick and Jessica Thompson, *Give Them Grace: Dazzling Your Kids with the Love of Jesus* (Wheaton, IL: Crossway, 2011).

and again (in one day), and at the end of that day, I just felt all out of forgiveness.

I walked upstairs to check on him and found his door closed, which is normally not the case. I could hear talking inside his room and started to jerk the door open, thinking he had his brother in there with him instead of getting ready for bed like I had asked. Thankfully, I realized that I was only hearing one voice, so I leaned my ear carefully against the door to hear him. He was praying, and his words took my breath away.

"Devil," he said, "you can't have me! I have Jesus on my side, and I won't let you steal from me or my family! Get away from me!"

Man, from the mouths of babes…

SOMETHING TO THINK ABOUT

As parents, there will be times when we feel fresh out of forgiveness, and the times when we probably most need to offer it to our children could be the times we least feel the ability to find it. That wasn't the only day I discovered my son praying truths I had taught him back to God or telling the enemy to leave him alone. It was a big truth; the devil does want to steal from our kids and our families, and we do have the authority to send him away. If I hadn't been willing in the past to offer my son truth and forgiveness, I'm not sure that moment would have happened.

Today's passage reminds us that God must've known we would struggle with overcoming sin. He must've foreseen that we would need grace not just once, but over and over, and that in order for us to extend that grace and forgiveness to others, we would first need to experience it ourselves…from Him. Only when we have deep understanding of how big and important God's forgiveness of us really is, will we have the strength we need to offer it to others.

Lord, increase our faith!

EXTRA VERSES FOR STUDY OR PRAYER

Mark 9:24; 2 Corinthians 5:7

VERSE OF THE DAY

And if he sins against you seven times in a day, and comes back to you seven times, saying, "I repent," you must forgive him. The apostles said to the Lord, "Increase our faith." —Luke 17:4–5

PRAYER

Father, help me to always remember how much I've been forgiven and let that knowledge of the depth of Your grace well over into my ability to forgive those around me. In Jesus's name, amen.

THINK

PRAY

PRAISE

TO-DO

PRAYER LIST

QUESTIONS FOR DEEPER REFLECTION

1. How often do you find yourself needing to forgive your children?

2. Do you ever run out of the ability to forgive them?

Day 13

PATIENCE IS REFUSING TO GIVE WAY

Now may the God who gives endurance and encouragement grant you to live in harmony with one another, according to Christ Jesus.
—Romans 15:5

Endurance is a long word, literally and figuratively. The word implies the ability to do something for a long time. Specifically, it means staying in an unpleasant or difficult process or situation without giving way.

If there was ever a job or calling that required endurance, it's motherhood. Stacey Thacker, in our co-written book *Unraveled*, says, "More and more I'm seeing motherhood as a marathon of endurance, not a sprint to the next stage of life…and in the marathon of motherhood, they hand you a person, not a baton…and you run it for life."[11] There really is no specific end to motherhood, and the requirements placed on moms when they're handed that little person often feel like they're just too heavy, especially with no end in sight.

In his letter to the Romans, Paul was talking to the church about the art of living together in harmony with believers in various stages of maturity. I can't think of a more important place for this to happen than inside the family, but I often find it more difficult to live in harmony with the people in my home than I do complete strangers! This is probably because we know each other so well, strengths and weaknesses, and with those things in mind, we have the ability to drive

---

11. Thacker and McGlothlin, *Unraveled*, 57.

each other crazy! I often have to remind myself that I'm the adult in this relationship because my emotions threaten to lower me to a level Christ has helped me rise above. It doesn't encourage harmony in our home for me forget everything God has taught me about looking and acting like Him, and yet I still find it hard.

So where do we get the ability to endure?

Romans 15:1 begins with a message for those *"who are strong."* I don't know where you are in your faith—if you're a new believer, a strong, seasoned, mature follower of Jesus, or somewhere in between—but I'm guessing you're further along in your faith than your children. According to this passage, mom, you are the one who is strong.

> *Now we who are strong have an obligation to bear the weaknesses of those without strength, and not to please ourselves. Each one of us is to please his neighbor for his good, to build him up.*
> (Romans 15:1–2)

SOMETHING TO THINK ABOUT

I know you don't always feel strong or feel like you have the ability to endure. Maybe you're reading this right now and wondering how you'll make it through the next five minutes, much less the teen years! I get that. I've felt it before, and I believe that no matter how old my children get, I'll always be called to endure with them.

But here's the secret: the ability to endure doesn't come from within me. Or you.

Look closely at today's verse. It says, *"Now may **the God who gives endurance** and encouragement **grant you to live in harmony** with one another, according to Christ Jesus."* Where does the ability to endure come from? Who grants us the gift, even the desire, to stay without giving way when this trait might not come naturally? God Himself.

This brings me so much comfort. In fact, every single time I remember that I don't have to be enough, have it all together, or even know everything there is to know about God, it brings me comfort. God is enough. God holds it all together. And God's character will never change. There's time for me to get to know Him and be changed *by* Him so I can lead my children *to* Him. This is why we must stay in prayerful relationship with the One who is the Giver of all good things, who offers us wisdom when we need it, and who helps us have compassion on those in our home who are weaker in the faith than we are.

EXTRA VERSES FOR STUDY OR PRAYER

Psalm 86:5; Romans 15:13

VERSE OF THE DAY

Now may the God who gives endurance and encouragement grant you to live in harmony with one another, according to Christ Jesus.   —Romans 15:5

PRAYER

Father, thank You for granting me everything I need. Help me remember that I don't have to possess it all within myself. My strength, my compassion, and my ability to endure through hard things comes through You, and Your well never runs dry. Give me what I need today. In Jesus's name, amen.

THINK

PRAY

PRAISE

_____

_____

TO-DO   PRAYER LIST

_____   _____

_____   _____

_____   _____

QUESTIONS FOR DEEPER REFLECTION

1. Have you ever had a moment when you felt like you just
    couldn't endure one second longer? What did you do?

_____

_____

2. Did you think to pray? Next time you feel this way, get
    alone with God, even for just for a few seconds, and ask
    Him to grant you what you need.

_____

_____

Day 14

PATIENCE IS THE FREEDOM TO GROW

For his anger lasts only a moment, but his favor, a lifetime.
Weeping may stay overnight, but there is joy in the morning.
—Psalm 30:5

It's one thing for us as moms to walk through hardships; it's something entirely different to watch our children walk through them.

When my family endured a recent hardship for one of our boys—waiting for answers, not knowing how things would turn out, and the massive effort to understand God's plan when it seemed to be leading in a direction completely opposite of our expectations—I felt like my emotions were getting tossed around like a boat in the middle of a storm. One moment, I would have peace, and the next moment, we'd get a new piece of information, and my peace felt like it fell overboard. I remember telling my Sunday school class that I looked forward to the season of my maturity in Christ, when it would take much more to toss me around, but I knew I had to go through this storm to get to the other side.

I often feel guilty about my need to fight, struggle, and strive to believe God when what I can see seems to contradict His truth. I've felt like I should be further along than I really am in my faith journey and wonder if it lets God down that I'm not. I want to be one of those devoted women of God who says earnestly and with sincere joy, "I will trust the Lord" while everything is falling apart around her. But the truth is that it takes me a few minutes, or sometimes a few weeks, to get there. I don't always have immediate joy or immediate faith, and I don't like that. I wish it weren't true, but I'm learning that it's the storm that strengthens us.

In John 11, we read the familiar story of Lazarus. After waiting several days to answer the desperate call of his friends for help, Jesus finally arrives at their home, only to find that Lazarus has already died. Lazarus's sister Mary had given up hope, and when Jesus does come, she does not immediately get up to greet Him. While the Scriptures don't give us specific insight into how she's feeling, I've always believed she was angry, struggling to understand and make sense of circumstances that didn't match what she had believed to be true.

I used to think she should have gotten up right away and run with her sister Martha to meet Jesus. After all, her king had arrived. Because I have the Bible, I knew what she didn't yet know: that Jesus was going to bring her brother back to life. It seems to me that she should've immediately wanted to be in His presence, trusting Him right away. But what her story demonstrates is that Mary—and others we discover in God's Word—was a lot more like me.

SOMETHING TO THINK ABOUT

The circumstances that finally brought Mary to Jesus's side cause me to pause. Do you know why? What was it that released her to take the first step toward trusting Him again?

He called for her. Martha told her, *"The Teacher is here and is calling for you"* (John 11:28).

When Mary heard that, she got up and ran to Him. Jesus could've been frustrated with her lack of maturity. He probably had the right to demand her allegiance regardless of how she felt. But Jesus offered Mary something entirely different—compassion, love, and patience.

He knew Mary couldn't see to the other side. She didn't know what miracle He was about to perform. All she could see was that her heart was broken, and the One who had the power to keep that from happening hadn't showed up on time. In response to her brokenness, the Scriptures say, "*he was deeply moved in his spirit and troubled*" (John 11:33). When He finally did see the place where Lazarus was laid, He wept.

It's so hard to trust God in the midst of trying circumstances, especially when we have little or no control over the outcome and can't see what's on the other side. Today's Scripture encourages us with the truth that joy will come. Hope will be restored. And it's okay for trust and faith to develop and grow with time.

EXTRA VERSES FOR STUDY OR PRAYER

Psalm 126:5; Isaiah 12:1

VERSE OF THE DAY

For his anger lasts only a moment, but his favor, a lifetime. Weeping may stay overnight, but there is joy in the morning.

—Psalm 30:5

PRAYER

Father, I am so limited, but You are a limitless God. Today, as I face the unknowns, help me to believe You will show up, and that when You do, it will be right on time. In Jesus's name, amen.

THINK

PRAY

PRAISE

_____

_____

TO-DO   PRAYER LIST

_____   _____

_____   _____

_____   _____

QUESTIONS FOR DEEPER REFLECTION

1. Have you ever struggled to trust God immediately when something happened that you couldn't understand?

_____

_____

2. Do you give yourself grace to grow in your faith? Or do you tend to beat yourself up for being less than perfect?

_____

_____

Day 15

PATIENCE IS LISTENING TO THE LORD'S CALL

In the morning, Lord, you hear my voice; in the morning I plead my case to you and watch expectantly. —Psalm 5:3

The text on the picture my husband sent me said, "Why should wake up at 4:30 a.m.," and I laughed out loud. (Not only is the idea of getting up that early hilarious to me, but whoever designed the graphic was clearly still groggy when they worked on it because they left out the word *you*. Case closed).

I'm not a morning person. In fact, it might be correct to say I really hate getting up early. I know doing so gives me several extra hours a week of productivity, and that it's the habit of highly successful people. I realize that it builds character and discipline, and that I'm more likely to get things done when there are fewer distractions. I even remember employing this method when I was in college— going to bed super early and waking up at the crack of dawn to study for a test right before taking it—but these pieces of information do nothing to change the fact that I don't want to get up early in the morning.

In all seriousness, many women have wondered whether there's something holy or sacred about spending time alone with the Lord in the morning. Some have even wondered if verses like today's make it a mandate that prayer and Bible study must happen before anything else. I've never believed that God's Word gives us this specific directive, but I do believe there's something special about giving God the first fruits of our morning (perhaps a bit later than 4:30).

There is a biblical pattern of rising early to get things done. We see it in the lives of Abraham, Moses, Joshua, Gideon, Samuel, David, and others. Jesus too. *"Very early in the morning, while it was still dark, he got up, went out, and made his way to a deserted place; and there he was praying"* (Mark 1:35). Shouldn't we follow His example? Or does the time for prayer matter?

The sweetest times of prayer I have come either very late at night or early in the morning. In fact, even though I have a habit of spending time in God's Word—and praying God's Word—first thing, I still go to sleep praying and wake up praying. It's a beautiful habit that developed in my forties when I started having difficulties with sleep.

The first few times it happened—probably the first few weeks—I grumbled and complained. There's nothing quite so frustrating as not being able to sleep. According to the Sleep Foundation, women have a lifetime risk of insomnia that is 40 percent higher than that of men.[12] Some have trouble falling sleep, while others having trouble *staying* asleep. Anyone who has experienced insomnia knows that the longer you go without sleeping, the more anxious and impatient you become. It's a cycle that made me extremely grumpy and fussy with the Lord. Of course, I took it out on Him in prayer. During that time, my prayers sounded like this:

- ⁜ "Lord, You have to let me sleep."

- ⁜ "Lord, please let me sleep."

- ⁜ "Lord, you know I'm an eight-hour-a-night kind of girl..."

- ⁜ "Lord, why would You do this? What's the point?"

- ⁜ "This is so not right. My husband is over there snoring. He fell asleep almost immediately."

- ⁜ "God, don't do this to me again!"

---

12. Eric Suni and Heather Wright, "Insomnia and Women," Sleep Foundation, January 25, 2023; www.sleepfoundation.org/insomnia/insomnia-women.

SOMETHING TO THINK ABOUT

My *ranting prayers* to the Lord weren't very pretty, but a few weeks in, I remembered the story of an older friend of mine who had struggled with sleep. She shared at a ministry meeting that she had been having trouble—waking up in the middle of the night, staying awake for a couple of hours, and then going back to sleep.

Instead of complaining about it, my friend thought maybe it was the Lord waking her up to pray. So she went with it. Setting her alarm for about the time she had been waking up, she rose quietly, slipped into an empty bedroom, and prayed. Then, after an hour or so had passed or she was finished praying, she would slip quietly back into bed and go back to sleep.

This inspired me. I didn't feel called to wake up in the middle of the night, but I did decide to give my waking time to the Lord. I began the habit of praying myself to sleep. I started with my husband and children, lifting up their specific needs, and then moved on to whomever the Lord allowed to pop into my mind next. The train of prayers, so to speak, went on and on until I fell asleep, not even worried about the time.

In the mornings, I began to set my alarm to go off fifteen minutes before I needed to get up and then setting a second alarm for *that* time. Eventually, I trained myself to hear the first alarm and almost immediately start to pray, usually beginning with prayers for my children and their days and then moving out to whatever or whomever the Lord placed on my heart from there. I expect Him to show me what to pray, and He faithfully answers.

Years later, this patient practice of prayer is one my most valuable, beloved habits. I get more accomplished for the kingdom when everyone else is asleep than I might the rest of the day because I trust that the Lord hears my voice.

EXTRA VERSES FOR STUDY OR PRAYER

Psalm 88:13; Psalm 130:5

VERSE OF THE DAY

In the morning, Lord, you hear my voice; in the morning I plead my case to you and watch expectantly.　　　—Psalm 5:3

PRAYER

Father, help me make the most of the time You give me. Help me to see annoying interruptions as potential calls to prayer for my family, my loved ones, and others You place in my path. Make me a faithful, patient prayer warrior for Your kingdom. In Jesus's name, amen.

THINK

PRAY

PRAISE

TO-DO

PRAYER LIST

QUESTIONS FOR DEEPER REFLECTION

1. Have you ever felt the Holy Spirit moving you to pray for someone? Describe what that felt like. Did you follow the nudge?

2. What would it be like for you to fill the quiet spaces of your life with prayer? This week, instead of trying to fill every lull with information or entertainment, allow yourself to be quiet and pray. If you need help knowing how to start, try doing what I do at night and in the morning. Start with your family and move on from there.

Part Two

WE CAN BE PATIENT BECAUSE OF WHO THE LORD IS

Day 16

THE LORD IS HOLY

Our Father which art in heaven, Hallowed be thy name.
—Matthew 6:9 (KJV)

When was the last time you stopped to really think about the fact that God is your Father and what that actually means for your daily life?

I have a great father, but my father did not have a great father. In fact, his earthly father abandoned him and his two brothers, leaving them destitute. My grandmother wrote to him often, begging him to help with shoes, medical bills, and other basic needs, but he didn't. At least not with any regularity. To make ends meet, she had to move back in with her parents for a time, an experience I'm sure was humbling and humiliating on some level.

Because they grew up fatherless and knew firsthand how important a father was to a family, my father and his two brothers decided to offer something different to their families. They were stayers, men who stayed. And with that decision, they taught me exactly what a good father does.

A good father takes care of his family.

A good father leads.

A good father protects.

A good father instructs.

A good father corrects.

A good father provides.

A good father loves.

When we pray the Lord's Prayer, we're praying to the Father who is all of these things and more. Even if our earthly father made mistakes and wasn't there for us, we still have the good news that our heavenly Father is all that we need, all of the time, without fail. He is our good Father.

But He's more than that.

A good earthly father might be praised, loved, esteemed, or even revered, but our heavenly Father should be hallowed.

The *Merriam-Webster Dictionary* defines hallowed as "holy, consecrated; sacred, revered." American theologian John Piper says hallow means to sanctify. "Sanctify can mean *make* holy or *treat as* holy. When God sanctifies us, it means that He makes us holy. But when we sanctify God, it means that we treat Him as holy."[13] When we first come to Christ, a transaction occurs that gives us the righteousness of Christ immediately. At the very moment we profess faith in Jesus, God no longer sees us as sinners, but as people who are covered in the righteousness of Christ. Christ was perfectly holy and now, because we are in Him, God sees us that way too.

But our holiness or sanctification also happens over time. As we pursue a deeper relationship with Jesus—reading the Bible, praying, walking in obedience—we change and slowly look more and more like Jesus spiritually. Allowing ourselves to be changed by God affects us on every level. When we treat Him as holy—believing Him, trusting Him, fearing Him over fearing man, hallowing Him, and keeping His commandments—He changes us into the image of Christ.

SOMETHING TO THINK ABOUT

I love to worship, especially with songs that remind me of who God is. Christians all over the world declare God's goodness, sovereignty, and holiness each Sunday and on other days throughout the

---

13. John Piper, "Hallowed Be Thy Name: In All the Earth," *Desiring God*, November 4, 1984; www.desiringgod.org/messages/hallowed-be-thy-name-in-all-the-earth.

week as we worship together corporately. But today's verse is referring to more than that.

It's a request.

It isn't believers declaring, "God, Your name is hallowed." No, it's believers asking God to make His name hallowed in our lives and in our circumstances, with the fullness of the meaning of that word in mind. In a beautiful way, our invitation to God to make much of His name in our lives is birthed from the realization that He *is holy*. One comes from the other. And really, God can't do otherwise. He is all about making His name great. He will make His name great. The beginning verse of the Lord's Prayer is us asking Him to make His name great in us.

We can be patient because God is at work in us. He will always make His name great, so we can trust Him with our lives.

EXTRA VERSES FOR STUDY OR PRAYER

First Samuel 2:2; Isaiah 6:3

VERSE OF THE DAY

Our Father which art in heaven, Hallowed be thy name.
—Matthew 6:9 KJV

PRAYER

Father, be hallowed in my life, in my heart, and in my home… today and every day. May my desire and choices to reverence You help my loved ones see me being made into Your image and believe You can do it in them too.

THINK

PRAY

PRAISE

TO-DO   PRAYER LIST

QUESTIONS FOR DEEPER REFLECTION

1. Did you have a good father?

2. How did (or does) your earthly father influence the way
    you see your heavenly Father? Even if your earthly father
    was good, take a minute to reflect on the ways you see God
    as being like him. Is this biblically accurate?

Day 17

THE LORD IS GOOD

Your kingdom come. Your will be done on earth as it is in heaven. —Matthew 6:10

I think one of the most profound truths God showed me in the midst of the craziness that was 2020 was the difference between praying for *my* kingdom to come and *His*.

I confess that probably over half the time when I pray, I'm asking God to build my kingdom—things I want, things I feel like I need, or things that would make my life easier somehow. I'm not saying it's wrong to ask God for what we need...as long as we remember that God is about the business of building His kingdom, not ours.

Elisabeth and Jim Elliot, together with four other couples, were missionaries to the Auca Indians, an extremely violent, completely unreached people group in Ecuador. After months of prepping, praying, and making small points of contact with the Aucas, the five men of the group—Jim, Pete Fleming, Nate Saint, Roger Youderian, and Ed McCully—landed their small plane near the Curaray River. They had hopes of being able to share the gospel that day.

Instead, all five men were speared to death by the Aucas.[14]

I've read the accounts leading up to and after that day, so I know this trip was covered in prayer, and the men believed they were firmly in God's will. I also know that all five wives were praying diligently for God to protect their husbands. They had young children who

---

14. Kristi Walker, "Who Were the Five Missionaries Who Died in the Ecuador Jungle?" Christianity.com, January 6, 2020; www.christianity.com/wiki/history/who-were-the-five-missionaries-who-died-in-the-ecuador-jungle.html.

needed their fathers. And yet, despite their pure plea, God said *no*. The answer to their prayers was no.

I listened to Elisabeth Elliot teach on the Lord's Prayer, and in that teaching, she shared some of her prayers and the conversations she had with God after Jim's death. The Elliots had a daughter who was just two when her father was murdered, and in one particular prayer, Elisabeth asked God why. Why would He choose to take a wonderful, godly father away from his toddler daughter, a daughter who probably wouldn't even be able to remember him? It seems like a reasonable question, one I know I would be tempted to ask if I found myself in Elisabeth's situation. But the answer that she felt God gave her was, "I am working on the bringing in of a kingdom, and I have a whole lot of other people in mind than just you and your fatherless child."

Wow. We think that sounds harsh, but it's true. And this perspective shift...realizing that we are such a small part of God's grand big plan, helps us offer our hearts to Him more freely. It also helps us be more okay with it when He says no or wait.

I find that when I get fussy with God over what I see as His lack of answer to my prayer, it's because I'm caring more about my kingdom than His. More about having my will done than His.

Elisabeth Elliot said, "It has been my experience that when I pray, 'Thy will be done,' it often involves the undoing of mine." That's true, but I would add that being able to pray, "Thy will be done" in the first place requires a level of trust in the idea that God is good, no matter what.

SOMETHING TO THINK ABOUT

Psalm 84:11 tells us that God will not withhold good from His children. That's comforting...but I wonder if we always trust God to define *good* for us.

As humans, we only see in part. God sees the full picture of how He is going to work *all* things together for good. (See Romans 8:28.)

In fact, sometimes we call things good that aren't good, or that hinder what God is trying to accomplish long-term. From our vantage point, verses like Psalm 84:11 can feel false—but they aren't.

However, if we have an incorrect understanding of our role in God's plan, or even that there is a bigger plan than what we can see, we'll struggle. God decides what is good. Faith places its trust in His judgment.

God will not withhold good from His children. And if He does withhold what we believed was good, it really wasn't His best.

We can be patient because we know God sees the big, eternal picture, and we know His heart for us is good.

EXTRA VERSES FOR STUDY OR PRAYER

Psalm 27:13; Psalm 84:11

VERSE OF THE DAY

Your kingdom come. Your will be done on earth as it is in heaven.   —Matthew 6:10

PRAYER

Father, help me to believe You are good, no matter what. So much of my impatience comes from wanting You to move faster or not liking it when You say no. Help me to trust You and widen my view of the way You're bringing Your kingdom to earth, so I can be a part of accomplishing it. In Jesus's name, amen.

THINK

PRAY

PRAISE

TO-DO

PRAYER LIST

QUESTIONS FOR DEEPER REFLECTION

1. What do you really think about the way Elisabeth Elliot felt God answered her question from today's devotion? Be honest. Does it rub you the wrong way?

2. Sometimes the truth—the bigger truth that goes way beyond our small circumstances, real and important as they may be—is hard to digest. Ask the Lord to help you see what you can't see. Share the truth of where you are with a trusted friend and ask them to pray that God will help you trust in His goodness no matter what.

Day 18

THE LORD IS FAITHFUL

Give us this day our daily bread. —Matthew 6:11 (ESV)

I like to think of this verse as a reminder of just how much we actually need God. For example, food and water are the most basic needs of mankind. We literally can't survive long without them, so in this verse, taken from the middle of the Lord's Prayer, as Jesus teaches us to ask for our daily bread, He's reminding us of just how much we need Him.

In today's pull yourself up by the bootstraps culture, we often find ourselves believing we don't need help. I'm not downplaying the entirely biblical notion of working to get the things we need. I used to have a sign on my fridge that quoted 2 Thessalonians 3:10 (NIV): *"The one who is unwilling to work shall not eat."* I meant to convey to my sons the importance of getting work done, finishing school, or cleaning up after themselves. At times, on weekends, I did withhold lunch from them until they got their work done. The ability and willingness to work hard is important, but in America, we take it a bit too far. There just doesn't seem to be much need for God because we can get almost everything we need without Him.

Until we can't.

Before I had kids, I had checked off every single life goal I had for myself. Every one. I knew I needed Jesus for salvation, but when my boys came along, I realized, like never before, that I didn't just need God...I desperately needed God. Every moment of every day, I needed God. I did not possess the kind of internal tools I needed to be the kind of mom I wanted to be, so I quickly learned to call on the

Lord in the middle of my days. Even just screaming, "Help me, Jesus!" made me feel like Jesus was indeed near and wanted to help. In fact, recognizing my need, plus the realization that I couldn't do this mom thing on my own, was what led me to prayer in the first place.

But there's more to this verse for us.

SOMETHING TO THINK ABOUT

In this part of the Lord's Prayer, Jesus is also reminding us that He is the giver of all good gifts. Every good thing we have is from Him. Notice that there is nothing God asks of us here. He doesn't say, "I'll give you your daily bread if you do this…" No, He just says we need to ask Him to give us the things we need.

But there is a catch, and I bet you already suspect what it is, right? You see, there's a difference between what we think we need and what God knows we need. In the hard parts of our days we might be tempted to think the thing we need the very most is for our finances to be in order, or our marriage difficulties to be healed. I'm not belittling those things, but they are temporal needs, not eternal needs. Praying for God to give us our daily bread implies that we'll accept whatever He provides.

The good news is that our God is the One who bends down to listen to us so that He can see and hear exactly what we need. (See Psalm 116:2.) But it's important to remember that you and I, our children, and our loved ones are not the only people on earth God is listening to, and it isn't our kingdom He's working to build. It's His. As believers, we are all part of a much bigger picture. We have to be able to look at whatever the Lord brings us in a day, good or bad, and trust that it's exactly what He wants us to have.

We can be patient because we know God sees our need and will meet it in His own good time.

EXTRA VERSES FOR STUDY OR PRAYER

Psalm 116:2; Lamentations 3:22–23

VERSE OF THE DAY

Give us this day our daily bread.   —Matthew 6:11 ESV

PRAYER

Father, help me to remember that You're not away in heaven, wondering what in the world is happening in my life. You are the God who bends down to listen. You hear my pleas, together with those of all Your children. I can trust Your provision. In Jesus's name, amen.

THINK

PRAY

PRAISE

TO-DO

PRAYER LIST

QUESTIONS FOR DEEPER REFLECTION

1. Are you ever tempted to think you don't need God?

2. Have you ever had a defining moment, a before-and-after event in which you knew with absolute clarity just how much you need God? Take a minute and describe why this event was a mercy to you.

Day 19

THE LORD IS FORGIVING

And forgive us our debts, as we also have forgiven our debtors.
—Matthew 6:12

When I was in graduate school, I wrote a long paper on the topic of forgiveness that examined its impact on our mental and emotional health. The research I found was astonishing but shouldn't come as much of a surprise to us as Christians. Holding on to unforgiveness, or even not asking for forgiveness, affects us on a biological level. It can cause stress, headaches, moodiness, or even disease. On a personal level, in our own homes, unforgiveness can keep us from treating someone the right way.

A couple of years ago, I had a come-to-Jesus meeting with my youngest son. This is the son who inspired much of my desperation as a new mom and who first taught me to fight for my sons instead of against them, so I hope that gives you a framework from which to picture the scene! He was in the recliner and I was sitting on the floor at his feet. I had given him a chance to explain his behavior, which had been very much below the expectations we have for him, when he told me he didn't understand why I was so upset with him.

Unknowingly, he had placed his finger on an open wound for me. I explained to him that the reason I took this kind of behavior so hard was because I felt like we'd been dealing with it for So. Many. Years. I reminded him that when he was five years old, he was a nightmare. I can't even count the number of times I carried him upstairs to his room—kicking, screaming, biting, and hitting me—to try to get him to calm down enough that he could even hear me. I can't count the times I sang to him through his tantrums, yelled "I love you!" over his screams, or held his little fists and feet so he couldn't hurt me.

As I told him these things, his mouth fell open more and more, and he finally said, "Mom, I never did that to you. Never. I would never treat you that way."

I stopped for what felt like an eternity to soak that in, and tears began to fall down my cheeks because I realized that he had no memory of those times that so defined my early motherhood. All of the times I labored over him, he can't even remember.

This was a powerful moment for me, and one where the Lord clearly showed me that I had held unforgiveness toward him in my heart for too long, for something that was covered, in the past, and hidden from everyone but me. Not only that, but my brokenness from that season was influencing the way I treated him now, and that wasn't fair to him. As far as he was concerned, it never happened. In his innocence, he reminded me of the way God removes our sin from us.

> As far as the east is from the west, so far has he removed our transgressions from us.   (Psalm 103:12)

SOMETHING TO THINK ABOUT

Unforgiveness can affect us on all levels, even more so because Jesus attaches a condition to this part of the Lord's Prayer. He says, "Forgive us our debts, as we also have forgiven our debtors." (Some Bible translations say we are to forgive sins or trespasses.) We have a tendency to downplay our sins and magnify those of people around us, but if this verse is true, it's just as important for us to forgive others as it is to ask for forgiveness ourselves.

As R. C. Sproul pointed out:

The why for forgiving others is rooted in the fact that we have been the recipients of extraordinary mercy and compassion. We are all debtors who cannot pay their debts to God.

Yet God has been gracious enough to grant us forgiveness in Jesus Christ. It is no wonder that in the Lord's Prayer, Jesus instructs His disciples to say, "Forgive us our debts as we forgive our debtors." There is a parallel, a joint movement of compassion, that is first received from God and then we in turn exercise the same compassion to others. God makes it clear that if we lack that compassion and harbor vengeance in our heart, rather than being ready to forgive again and again, we will forfeit any forgiveness that has been given to us.[15]

As women of God, we need to learn to keep short accounts with God, to go to Him daily to ask Him to forgive us when we need it and help us forgive others, especially those who live in our homes. We can be patient and offer forgiveness to others because we know what it cost God to forgive us.

EXTRA VERSES FOR STUDY OR PRAYER

Psalm 32:5; Psalm 103:11

VERSE OF THE DAY

And forgive us our debts, as we also have forgiven our debtors.
—Matthew 6:12

PRAYER

Father, I confess that I find it hard to forgive. In fact, I know that even if I do choose to forgive, I might have to do it again…and again. Help me to trust You with this and offer forgiveness to others with the same grace and magnitude You offer it to me. In Jesus's name, amen.

---

15. R. C. Sproul, "Why Forgive?" Ligonier Ministries, January 31, 2022; www.ligonier.org/learn/articles/why-forgive.

THINK

PRAY

PRAISE

TO-DO

PRAYER LIST

QUESTIONS FOR DEEPER REFLECTION

1. As you read today's devotion, did God lay someone on your heart whom you need to forgive?

2. Take stock. What is it costing you to hold on to any unforgiveness you might have?

Day 20

THE LORD WILL HELP
US STAND

And lead us not into temptation, but deliver us from evil.
—Matthew 6:13 (ESV)

Several years ago, when my boys were very small, I had a habit of sneaking into their rooms to pray for them. They shared a room at the time, so I would sit on the floor beside their bunk beds and lay hands on them, each in turn, to pray for specific things I wanted God to do in their lives. Any mom can relate to the concept of having devils by day and angels by night. No matter how challenging our children have been during their waking hours, there's just something about seeing them asleep that grabs a mother's heart.

One evening, I was particularly overcome by how innocent and precious they looked while they slept. I started to weep and beg God to keep them from evil. The pure sight I saw in front of me just broke my heart, and the idea that the world was coming for them very soon made me want to stand in front of them and physically protect them.

The next morning, I attended a women's Bible study. We started out in small groups in which we would discuss the previous week's material and pray for each other. During my time to talk, I shared what had happened as I prayed for my boys the night before.

One mom whose children were much older and on their own, spoke up in response to my story, and what she shared has stuck with me ever since. She said, "You're praying for the wrong thing, Brooke. They are going to see and experience evil in this world, and it isn't wrong to pray that God will spare them some of it. But they are going to be tempted. Your prayer needs to be that when they encounter evil, when they are tempted, they'll stand firm."

What is this evil?

Specifically, according to the original Greek, the evil that Jesus is referring to in the Lord's Prayer is the evil one, Satan himself, not just evil in general. I've been telling my boys for what seems like their entire lives that the enemy is not their friend. John 10:10 says, "A thief [Satan] comes only to steal and kill and destroy." Satan's job is to mess us up. Now, as teenagers, if I ask them what Satan's job is, those words will easily roll off their tongues, but I wanted this to be a central truth of their lives. God is for you, and Satan is against you.

In Genesis 4:7 (ESV), right in the middle of the story of Cain and Abel, God tells Cain, "*If you do well, will you not be accepted? And if you do not do well, sin is crouching at the door. Its desire is contrary to you, but you must rule over it.*" I used to sit on the floor with my boys, point to the door frame, and say, "See that door? Satan is behind it, and he wants you. You have to fight him off." When they were super little, they would get up to go look behind the door to see if this Satan was actually there. I explained to them that Satan doesn't look like we think he does, and he isn't always obvious or easy to see. The imagery here is that there is an enemy who is literally waiting like a crouching lion just around the corner, watching and waiting for the right time to spring into action. (See 1 Peter 5:8.)

SOMETHING TO THINK ABOUT

When Jesus taught His disciples to ask God to deliver them from evil in the Lord's Prayer, He wasn't just telling them to say, "Lord, protect me." He was telling them to be aware that there really is an enemy of our souls whose only job is our destruction. We need to ask God to protect us from his schemes and give us strength to stand in our faith when we are tempted.

My fifteen-year-old asked me once why Satan was so interested in Christians. I thought it was a great question. After all, wouldn't Satan be more interested in trying to keep non-Christians from coming to Christ? Seems like he would do better to focus on them than on us. The answer to this question is that as much as God wants to use our lives to display His love to the people we influence, including those closest to us, Satan wants to use us the same way. How much better would it be, from Satan's perspective, to destroy a believer's life in front of the people he or she influences so it appears to non-Christians that Jesus isn't worth following?

We can be patient because God wants to use us as living testimonies of His love and provision to those He wants to save.

EXTRA VERSES FOR STUDY OR PRAYER

Exodus 34:6; Numbers 14:18

VERSE OF THE DAY

And lead us not into temptation, but deliver us from evil.
—Matthew 6:13 ESV

PRAYER

Lord, be our shield against this world. When temptations come, give us the strength to stand. Help us love You so well that those in our homes and those around the world will be drawn to You. In Jesus's name, amen.

THINK

PRAY

_____

_____

PRAISE

_____

_____

TO-DO   PRAYER LIST

_____

_____

QUESTIONS FOR DEEPER REFLECTION

1. Have you ever thought to pray for your son or daughter to stand firm when they're tempted? How does it make you feel to know they will be tempted, and that you can't stop it?

_____

_____

2. Are there ways God is calling you to resist temptation?

_____

_____

Day 21

THE LORD IS JUST

If we confess our sins, he is faithful and just to forgive us our sins and to cleanse us from all unrighteousness. —1 John 1:9 (ESV)

"It's not fair!"

Every child has screamed these three words at some point in their life. I used to be the fair police when I was a child. I remember saying it quite often when I perceived a friend had received more food than I did or got to play with a toy longer. Now, as a mother of teenagers, I hear these three words said in different ways:

+ "You let him off too easily."
+ "You never give him the same punishments you give me."
+ "I would never have gotten away with that."

My boys are close in age—twenty-three months apart—and when they were little, I was tempted to treat them exactly the same. They were born within what seemed to be such a short time frame that it often felt like I was parenting one unit of children instead of two separate boys. In fact, in the beginning, I think I missed out on some of their uniqueness because I thought they were so much alike. Turns out, they were quite different and needed different forms of parenting to meet their needs.

Now, years later, I sometimes get accused of treating them differently...because I do! I don't always correct or discipline them in the exact same way. The Bible doesn't give a lot of specific guidance for parents, which leads me to believe I have a lot of freedom in the way

I try to reach their hearts. And while it may not seem fair to them in the moment, I know the truth.

They don't really want what's fair.

I served for many years in crisis pregnancy centers. As part of my time in the counseling room, if the door opened, I would share the gospel. I didn't do it with every single client—sometimes the door to a woman's soul was firmly closed—but I did try to share at least a part of the good news with every woman, even if it just meant showing unconditional love. If the Lord made a way, my gospel presentation, and the conversation I had with the woman on the couch in front of me, often went something like this:

> Imagine you're in a courtroom, about to go in front of the judge for crimes you know you're guilty of. You have no doubt about your guilt. In fact, your guilt has already been proven beyond a reasonable doubt. All that remains now is to receive your punishment.
>
> The judge walks into the courtroom, and a hush falls over everyone there. You see a man you don't know walk in and approach the judge. They talk quietly for a few moments, each asking and answering questions, and then the man turns to leave.
>
> The judge looks at you and says, "You are guilty of this crime. But this Man, the One who just walked into the courtroom, has taken the punishment you deserved. Every ounce of what you deserved, He will take on himself. He said He loves you and of His own free will, He took your punishment upon Himself. It is finished. You are free to go."

At this point, the woman I was serving that day would almost always say something like, "That isn't fair!" And my reply? "I know. It isn't."

SOMETHING TO THINK ABOUT

God is a just God. He does everything right and doesn't make mistakes. According to Acts 10:34, He doesn't show partiality, and He hates the mistreatment of those the world sees as less than perfect. The extension of that justness, that fairness, is that when we sin (and we all sin), He is also committed to giving us what we deserve. We all deserve hell. That's why what Jesus did on the cross is such a big deal. That's why when I share the illustration of the Man in the courtroom, it seems unfair, but the truth is that God's perfect justice was meted out on His perfect Son. We don't have to get justice for our sins because Jesus already took that punishment for us. It isn't fair, but we don't really want what's fair.

Neither do our children.

But we do have to put our faith in what Jesus did for us on the cross for it to apply to our accounts. Jesus made the offer. The work is done. We just have to believe it, accept it, and then live out of love and gratitude toward Him every day for the rest of our lives.

We can be patient because we serve a God who is just, who doesn't give us what we deserve because of what Jesus did on the cross.

EXTRA VERSES FOR STUDY OR PRAYER

Acts 10:34; Romans 3:23

VERSE OF THE DAY

If we confess our sins, he is faithful and just to forgive us our sins and to cleanse us from all unrighteousness. —1 John 1:9 ESV

PRAYER

Father, thank You for making a way for me. I don't deserve to be pardoned for my sin. My sin is great and deserving of hell, but You have offered me something different. Help me to live like I believe it today, Lord. And may my children see Your grace at work in me. In Jesus's name, amen.

THINK

PRAY

PRAISE

TO-DO

PRAYER LIST

QUESTIONS FOR DEEPER REFLECTION

1. When was the last time you felt like something happened to you that just wasn't fair?

2. Unfair things happen to us all the time. How does remembering what Jesus did for you on the cross change your attitude about this?

Day 22

THE LORD IS GRACIOUS

The LORD is compassionate and gracious, slow to anger and abounding in faithful love. —Psalm 103:8

I wonder if we could handle it if we could actually see how gracious God is to us? As a young adult, I often pondered Ephesians 6:12, which says, *"For our struggle is not against flesh and blood, but against the rulers, against the authorities, against the cosmic powers of this darkness, against evil, spiritual forces in the heavens."* Were there actual invisible evil spirits at war all around me? Were God's angels defending me and all of God's children in some epic spiritual battle? What if I could see it happening? Would my very human self be able to take it all in? Would it be too much for me? Perhaps that's why God doesn't allow us to see it, only to know it's happening.

Certainly, part of God's graciousness is to keep us from seeing things that would be too much for us to process and to make provisions for us against the seen and unseen war for our hearts. We have an enemy whose only job is to kill, steal, and destroy, and the Lord fights for His people. (See, respectively, John 10:10; Exodus 14:14.) But God's gracious demeanor toward us isn't just about keeping us from harm. It's also about being generous, courteous, kind, and pleasant.

Is that how you see God? Your generous provider? Respectful and considerate of your needs? Kind and loving? Pleasant to be around? Some see Him as a harsh taskmaster, a God who demands obedience and cracks the whip. God is holy and glorious, and He does require our obedience. When you and I said yes to Jesus, we gave Him the right to do with our lives whatever He wants. That means our task is to cooperate with whatever He brings our way. He's our Creator, so He has the right to ask for those things. But there is so much more to God than just this!

- If He were only a demanding God, He would be cruel. He is not cruel.

- If He were only a demanding God, He would be cold. He is not cold.

- If He were only a demanding God, He would seem distant. He is not distant.

God's true nature is far beyond just being demanding. He is:

- Compassionate, meaning He cares deeply for the challenges we face

- Patient, waiting to mature us in the right time and putting up with our mistakes along the way

- Slow to anger, not giving us what our sins deserve

- Absolutely overflowing with faithfulness and pure love

  And yes, gracious.

SOMETHING TO THINK ABOUT

If I had to make a list of all the ways God has been gracious to me just this morning, it would look something like this:

- I woke up in a warm bed, with my husband beside me.

- Both of my children woke up and are healthy.

- I had enough food to feed myself and my family this morning.

- We were able to open the Bible together around the breakfast table before my children went to school.

- We had enough gas in the car to get where we needed to go.

- I had hot water to take a shower.

- I had electricity to help me get ready for the day.

+ I had clothing to keep me covered and warm.

+ I had access to a Bible and a comfortable couch to sit on while I read it and prayed.

+ I had pens and paper for note-taking and recording what God has been teaching me.

+ I have a computer and access to the Internet, which allows me to follow God's will for this season of my life.

+ I had enough leftovers from dinner last night to eat for lunch.

+ I have friends who can help me get things done when I can't get them done myself.

And that's just the grace that God extended to me before noon. Others will find countless ways that He extends His grace.

We can be patient and trust the Lord with our lives because God offers us so much grace.

EXTRA VERSES FOR STUDY OR PRAYER

Exodus 34:6; Numbers 14:18

VERSE OF THE DAY

The LORD *is compassionate and gracious, slow to anger and abounding in faithful love.*　　—Psalm 103:8

PRAYER

Father, thank You for being so kind and gracious to me. Give my family eyes to see Your kindnesses to us today, even and especially in the little things, so that we can find the faith to believe You in the bigger things. In Jesus's name, amen.

THINK

_____

_____

PRAY

_____

_____

PRAISE

_____

_____

TO-DO   PRAYER LIST

_____

_____

QUESTIONS FOR DEEPER REFLECTION

1. Make a list like mine that includes all of the ways you can think of that God has been gracious to you so far today.

_____

2. God is making provisions for you and your loved ones all the time, working all things together for your good. Tonight over dinner, or the next time your entire family is together, ask everyone to share one way the Lord has been gracious to them that day. Be prepared to go first to demonstrate what it looks like.

_____

Day 23

THE LORD IS UNCHANGING

For I the Lord do not change; therefore you, O children of Jacob, are not consumed. —Malachi 3:6 (esv)

Nothing has ever challenged my organizational skills like surviving graduate school.

I made it all the way through high school and college before I ever had a calendar or wrote important dates on anything other than my course syllabus. When I hit graduate school, all of that changed. I made it through the first couple weeks of school before any assignments were due, with little stress and little fear of what could go wrong. I had been a good student all of my life; my systems, what few of them I did have, had always served me well. Then, one morning, as I sat in one of my favorite classes with Dr. Gene Mastin, he reminded us that a large assignment was due in less than a week. On top of that, he held up a copy of the book we were reading and showed us about where we should be in it if we had hopes of writing the chapter summaries on time.

Now, I was stressed.

I realized, in a rather panicked way, that I was already so far behind on my assignments that I might not be able to catch up. I didn't do it intentionally, and I wasn't a lazy student. I had just forgotten to look at the syllabus dates. As a result, I had a big problem.

After falling completely apart on the phone with my dad, I drove to the nearest office supply store and bought one of those huge desk calendars, plus another calendar that fit inside of my main class binder. Then, I went back to my apartment, sat on the floor with all four of my class syllabi surrounding me, and made a plan. I started with writing the due dates on the biggest calendar and then worked backward, designing a schedule for all of the individual parts and pieces of the assignments that would allow me to get them done well in advance. I lived by those schedules for the entire two years it took me to get done with my course load. Today, I credit that moment of panic for propelling me toward taking control of my life and learning how to successfully get things done.

Now, twenty-some years later, I still write things down to remember them. I use a physical day planner in which I can pencil in important information because in the age of electronics, it helps me stay on top of my days. If I don't write an event or due date down, it doesn't happen. I don't always strategically plan out every single step of my current life assignments anymore but I do plan out each day, blocking time for important things on my to-do list so that they aren't forgotten.

In the book of Malachi, God's people had forgotten. Specifically, they had forgotten how much God loved them and had lost their fear of their Creator.

SOMETHING TO THINK ABOUT

God sent the prophet Malachi to the nation of Israel to give them a stern reminder.

- They had lost their love for God.
- They were disgracing His name.
- They were breaking His covenants and then expecting His blessing in return.

They thought God was just like them—able to disregard their sins as if they didn't matter. They thought He would overlook their offenses and still bless them when they asked for it. In a similar but less eternally damaging way, I did the same thing at the beginning of graduate school. I thought I could get by with the same effort I'd put forth in my previous schooling and thought that God would bless my efforts in the same way He always had. But God is not like us in that way. He doesn't overlook sin, and He doesn't miss opportunities to help us grow. In fact, one of the most comforting parts of God's character is that He does *not* change.

Could it be that part of the reason we feel impatient with the Lord and His timing in our own lives and in the lives of our children is because we've forgotten that God doesn't change?

Yesterday, we examined the truth that God is not only a taskmaster, demanding obedience and cracking the whip, but He is also holy, glorious, kind, courteous, generous, and loving toward His children. He does demand obedience, but He doesn't change. He is God, "*the faithful God who keeps his gracious covenant loyalty for a thousand generations with those who love him and keep his commands*" (Deuteronomy 7:9).

We can be patient because we serve the God who doesn't change, whose faithfulness lasts for generations, and whose plans for us are good.

EXTRA VERSES FOR STUDY OR PRAYER

Deuteronomy 7:9; Psalm 102:27

VERSE OF THE DAY

For I the LORD *do not change; therefore you, O children of Jacob, are not consumed.* —Malachi 3:6 (ESV)

PRAYER

Father, help my family to fear You above all else, reverencing Your name, remembering Your great love and care for us, and putting our faith in Your character. Give us comfort in the knowledge that who You have always been is who You will continue to be. May our decisions to honor You come from that place. In Jesus's name, amen.

THINK

PRAY

PRAISE

TO-DO   PRAYER LIST

QUESTIONS FOR DEEPER REFLECTION

1. Allow me to take the message today one step further. I don't just think the reason we find it difficult to be patient is because we've forgotten God's character. I think the reason we find walking out the Christian life, in all its parts, difficult is because we routinely forget who God is. The purpose of this second part of the journal is to remind us of just that. Which of God's character traits that you've already studied has been most important to you so far?

2. What are some practical ways you and your family can remember who God is? Check out Million Praying Moms (www.millionprayingmoms.com) for help with this.

THE LORD IS ALL-KNOWING

Lord, you have searched me and known me. You know when I sit down and when I stand up; you understand my thoughts from far away. You observe my travels and my rest; you are aware of all my ways. —Psalm 139:1–3

Personally, one of the hardest parts of walking out my faith is the unknown. In so many ways, our faith is blind, and yet God asks us to trust in what we can't see, knowing that He sees all.

I once worked for a CEO who told me he wanted to constantly live in a space where if God didn't show up, nothing happened. I didn't like that at first. It seemed way too risky and uncertain to the young woman I was back then. I wanted to be sure. I wanted to see a clear path forward, and I wanted to know exactly what that path would entail.

What my CEO meant was that he wanted to be fully committed and dependent upon God, to live in such a way that his entire existence, victory, and success depended upon God keeping His promises. I believed in the promises of God; I was just very shortsighted in my faith and lacked the experience with God to trust Him fully. I knew Proverbs 3:5–6 (ESV) said, *"Trust in the Lord with all your heart, and do not lean on your own understanding. In all your ways acknowledge him, and he will make straight your paths."*

I trusted God with all the heart I knew to give Him in that season, but I didn't realize the path would most likely come to me just one step at a time, or that God might ask me to step out in faith, not knowing where I was going.

I've never forgotten the heart of that message of purposeful dependence upon the promises of God, and there's never been an area of my life when I've felt it more than motherhood. Prayer is the intersection of a mother's heart and God's provision. It's her wild and free declaration that if God doesn't show up, nothing happens.

+ She knows there are no formulas for raising good, godly kids.

+ She knows that even her very best could still fail to be enough.

+ She knows she can't control everything that comes into her children's lives.

+ She knows she can trust God to see the right path and keep her family on it.

+ She knows she is desperate for the goodness of God, and she can trust Him to keep His promises, even if she can't see them right now or has to wait to see the fruit of her prayers and hard work.

+ She knows that she doesn't know it all…so she prays to the God Who does.

SOMETHING TO THINK ABOUT

King David, who wrote today's passage and many other psalms, was a man who made many decisions, both good and bad, without knowing what would happen on the other side. Here are just a few of the better ones:

+ He was anointed king and then served in the palace of King Saul, not knowing how he would be received or when he would take the throne.

+ He took on the giant Philistine Goliath with just a few stones and a sling, charging forward with full faith in what God *could* do but not knowing for sure what He *would* do.

+ He ran from Saul's presence and made his home in caves after Saul tried to kill him multiple times.

✦ He chose not to kill Saul when he had the opportunity because that would have dishonored God.

There are countless other biblical characters who chose to trust in their all-knowing God without knowing much themselves. Abraham, Sarah, Paul, Ananias, and many others put their faith in God in spite of the personal cost—and God took care of them. When I'm tempted to play it safe or stress because I don't know or can't control what's coming next for my family, I think about these stories, and I'm filled with faith. I remember what I do know and pray for God to take care of what I don't.

We can be patient because God already knows what's next, and we can trust His promises to be good.

EXTRA VERSES FOR STUDY OR PRAYER

Genesis 15:13–16; Acts 9:10–19

VERSE OF THE DAY

Lord, you have searched me and known me. You know when I sit down and when I stand up; you understand my thoughts from far away. You observe my travels and my rest; you are aware of all my ways. —Psalm 139:1–3

PRAYER

Father, I confess that I don't like not knowing. I wish I could see the big picture in the same way You can. I know You are growing my faith muscle, Lord, and I know I can trust You with what I can't see. Help me to remember what I know to be true about You and make me like the men and women of the Bible who put their faith in You. In Jesus's name, amen.

THINK

_____

_____

PRAY

_____

_____

PRAISE

_____

_____

TO-DO

_____

_____

_____

PRAYER LIST

_____

_____

_____

QUESTIONS FOR DEEPER REFLECTION

1. Is there something God is asking you to trust Him in or for right now?

_____

_____

2. What's holding you back from walking in obedience? Read some of the extra verses for study or prayer and ask God to fill you with all the faith you need to do what He's called you to do.

_____

_____

Day 25

THE LORD HOLDS ALL
THINGS TOGETHER

For everything was created by him, in heaven and on earth, the
visible and the invisible, whether thrones or dominions or rulers or
authorities—all things have been created through him and for him.
He is before all things, and by him all things hold together.

—Colossians 1:16–17

When my children were very young, I distinctly remember feeling like I had to hold it all together, and by that, I mean hold everything together—the family schedule, the state of the house, the laundry, my job, the children's survival, my emotions, the meals, grocery shopping, and on and on. I don't mean to imply in any way that my husband didn't serve our family. He did. In fact, he is one of the most hands-on dads I know. But his heavy involvement in our children's lives didn't erase the fact that I felt everything depended upon me. I'm guessing you can relate. Even now that I have teenagers who are much more self-sufficient and able to contribute to the family, I still feel like I'm the one keeping all of the plates spinning in the air, and that if I quit, everything will come crashing down.

I remember one specific evening that it came to a head. My poor husband came home from work to find the house a disaster—no dinner cooked and a wife who'd been run ragged by the young children that day. I know he didn't mean to insult me or add to my pressure, but his comments about these things made me feel like he was disappointed in me. In fact, to this day, when he makes a comment about the house being messy, I take it personally. I can't seem to help it. He's just making a statement—and a true one at that!—but when I feel the weight of responsibility, even though I work almost as much as he does, it's personal.

Add to this the fact that my mother-in-law worked full-time outside of her home for most of his life, had three children, and still managed to keep an immaculate home. She was superwoman and raised an amazing man, but I felt inferior to her in this way, like I would never live up to that standard. That particular night, I told him exactly how I felt. I made it known that I couldn't possibly hold everything together the way he wanted me to, and that I might never be able to be the wife and mother he wanted me to be. I also told him he'd need to make peace with that because my very best efforts were still falling short.

Poor guy. He didn't really deserve my words that night, and he had never told me he wanted me to be anything other than what I was. He just caught me falling apart.

SOMETHING TO THINK ABOUT

If ever there was a person who deserved to feel like everything was falling apart, it was the apostle Paul as he wrote the letter to the Colossians. Classified as a prison epistle, Paul's letter to the early church at Colossae was written while he was imprisoned in Rome for the first time. In fact, Paul wrote several letters during that prison stay, including Ephesians, Philippians, and Philemon. I suppose we could call that making the best out of a bad situation!

Paul believed that every circumstance he encountered, whether in plenty or in want, was given to him directly from God. He learned to trust God or be content in all of them. He knew it was God who held his life together, not him.

Can I repeat that to all of the moms reading this who have felt the same way I have at times? You are not the one holding it all together. God is. Yes, I know you have responsibilities and items on your to-do list that must get done but let go of the pressure to be something you weren't meant to be. God is holding you together, mama.

My friend and fellow author Stacey Thacker writes:

We can be overwhelmed by the truth of who Jesus is instead of being overwhelmed by life. We can hold together knowing He is able. He is unshakable. He can handle whatever our day brings.[16]

Even in the worst circumstances and the hardest, most challenging days, He's the One who's in charge. It's His mighty, strong, capable hands that hold us.

Like Paul in prison, be focused on who God is instead of where you are. Trust that wherever He has you right now, He's there with you, ready to meet you and help you handle it all. We can be patient and let go of the pressure to get it all right because God is holding our lives together.

EXTRA VERSES FOR STUDY OR PRAYER

Psalm 63:8; Philippians 4:13

VERSE OF THE DAY

For everything was created by him, in heaven and on earth, the visible and the invisible, whether thrones or dominions or rulers or authorities—all things have been created through him and for him. He is before all things, and by him all things hold together.

—Colossians 1:16–17

PRAYER

Father, I can't help but feel like I'm the one holding it all together for my family, but Your Word says I'm not. I know my role as a mom is important but help me to see myself as I truly am—fully supported by Your strong, mighty hands. In Jesus's name, amen.

---

16. Stacey Thacker and Brooke McGlothlin, *Hope for the Weary Mom: Let God Meet You in the Mess* (Eugene, OR: Harvest House Publishers, 2012), 110.

THINK

_____

_____

PRAY

_____

_____

PRAISE

_____

_____

TO-DO   PRAYER LIST

_____   _____

_____   _____

_____   _____

QUESTIONS FOR DEEPER REFLECTION

1. Confess. When was the most recent time you felt the pressure to get it all right or hold everything together for your family?

_____

_____

2. The feelings that come with this pressure are suffocating, but the knowledge that God has us firmly settled in His capable hands brings with it an entirely different feeling. What is that for you?

_____

_____

THE LORD IS WISE

Now if any of you lacks wisdom, he should ask God—who gives to all generously and ungrudgingly—and it will be given to him. —James 1:5

There can be no doubt that raising children today is drastically different than it was for my parents in the 1990s. The issues might be similar—questions about identity, emotional responses, influence, peer pressure, and academics—but the way kids today have to deal with these was forever changed by technological advances and the Internet. I often hear frustration from moms trying their best to navigate a world they didn't have access to when they were children.

If another kid was mean to me in high school, at least I had the sanctuary of my home to get away from them for an evening, a weekend, or the summer. Now, mean kids follow our kids into our homes, into their bedrooms, and into the deepest recesses of their hearts. Everything they do has the potential to be recorded and shared everywhere. One simple misstep or fall can follow our children forever through photos, videos, comments, emojis, or memes. Their feelings of value and self-worth can get bogged down by how many people like or view what they share.

It's no wonder us moms often find ourselves not knowing what to do. I can't tell you the number of times my two children have brought an issue home that my husband and I really didn't know how to handle because we never went through it the way they are. Parenting in the technology age has brought with it an entirely new set of challenges. We are pioneers, my friends—pioneers who have to trust in the Word of God now more than ever.

No, there's no book of the Bible, no chapter or verse, that tells us how much screen time our middle schoolers should have or whether our seventeen-year-old should have access to her phone at night in her bedroom. There's no rule section in Revelation that says what video games they should be allowed to play. And frankly, there is no long-term research to show how all of this will affect their brains as they mature into adults. It's scary. About 99.9 percent of the time, I feel a complete lack of wisdom. I simply don't know what to do.

That's why I'm so grateful for today's verse. The first seven words, *"Now if any of you lacks wisdom"* makes it clear that God is speaking directly to me. Hand raised high, friend, I need all the wisdom I can get! Praise God for the rest of the verse, which gives me the comfort of knowing God doesn't leave me there. My God says all I have to do is ask Him for wisdom, and He, as the author of wisdom, will give it to me. And not just give a little...oh no, my God gives wisdom generously and without reservation to His beloved children.

Could there be any better news for parents than this?

SOMETHING TO THINK ABOUT

Oh, the depth of the riches and the wisdom and the knowledge of God! How unsearchable his judgments and untraceable his ways! (Romans 11:33)

Dear friend, it isn't just that the Lord knows more than we do. It's that He knows better. He knows all. To me, one of the most exciting parts of being a woman of prayer, a praying mom, is that I serve the God who will give me what I need to do what He's called me to do.

Recently, my prayers asking for wisdom have been short and sweet. Two words are my plea to the God of unsearchable wisdom:

Show me.

Show me, Lord, what my next step should be. Show me, Lord, the right path for my child. Show me, Lord, how to meet this need. Show me, Lord, what things are hidden that I need to see.

Lord, show me.

EXTRA VERSES FOR STUDY OR PRAYER

Proverbs 3:19–20; Romans 11:33

VERSE OF THE DAY

Now if any of you lacks wisdom, he should ask God—who gives to all generously and ungrudgingly—and it will be given to him. —James 1:5

PRAYER

Show me, Lord. Give me wisdom in this moment, for this day, and for such a time as this. Help me remember to ask for it and wait for it. For Your wisdom is more and so much better than mine. In Jesus's name, amen.

THINK

PRAY

PRAISE

TO-DO

PRAYER LIST

QUESTIONS FOR DEEPER REFLECTION

1. Have you ever felt at a complete loss with your children or loved ones who lean on you for wisdom?

2. Try putting today's verse into practice on a moment-by-moment basis. When you need wisdom, but don't have it, pray, "Show me, Lord." It might not happen right away, but according to God's Word, it will. Trust it! Wait for it!

Day 27

THE LORD IS LOVING

Haven't I commanded you: be strong and courageous? Do not be afraid or discouraged, for the LORD your God is with you wherever you go. —Joshua 1:9

His big brown eyes looked up into mine; he was afraid and full of questions. After four years of homeschooling—the only thing he'd ever known—my youngest son and his big brother were going to school. Big brother, the social butterfly, was raring to go, ready to make new friends and face new adventures. But my little guy was not so sure about this change. In fact, he had asked me the night before if he was being punished. Had he done something bad to be sent away from me? And why wasn't his daddy living with us anymore? Had he been bad?

Rest assured; nothing was wrong in my marriage. We had moved, and my husband didn't get a transfer in his job as early as we'd hoped. In fact, the boys and I lived a full year without him. Our two sons—those loud, aggressive, impulsive, all-boy sons—were used to having access to their dad whenever they wanted him, so they found it hard to function without him. For the first time ever, I felt the Lord leading us to take a different path educationally. As hard as it was for my youngest son to understand, it was harder for me to let him go. The night before I dropped him off at school for the first time, he cried as I put him to bed. Every night thereafter for at least a month, he crawled into my bed with me and told me how much he missed his dad.

What he needed was reassurance of my presence. He wanted to know I was near, and he was loved. His security came from my unchanging love and care for him. In the absence of everything he knew, everything that had previously given him stability, he needed to be close to what was the same.

Thankfully, the Lord provided this son with a group of good friends, so after just a few weeks' time, he looked forward to going to school. He also learned how to function in a classroom.

My heart still aches over it a bit, if I'm honest. I still feel like a homeschooling mom whose kids happen to be in public school. During the time we were adjusting as a family, when my son needed to be close to me, I also needed to be close to what was true and familiar.

I needed to be close to God. I needed to know that I was loved.

SOMETHING TO THINK ABOUT

In the first chapter of the book of Joshua, we find that Moses, the man who led God's people to the promised land, has died, and Joshua had been chosen to take his place. In the transition, as God told His people to enter the land He had given to them, He gave them a reminder that was designed to give them assurance of His care.

> **Be strong and courageous**, for you will distribute the land I swore to their ancestors to give them as an inheritance. Above all, **be strong and very courageous** to observe carefully the whole instruction my servant Moses commanded you. Do not turn from it to the right or the left, so that you will have success wherever you go. This book of instruction must not depart from your mouth; you are to meditate on it day and night so that you may carefully observe everything written in it. For then you will prosper and succeed in whatever you do. Haven't I commanded you: **be strong and courageous**? Do not be afraid or discouraged, for the Lord your God is with you wherever you go.   (Joshua 1:6–9)

On the morning that my brown-eyed boy left me to go to school for the first time, I recited Joshua 1:9 to him. In fact, I had bought him a shirt with that verse on it, and he wore it often. I reminded him that even though I couldn't be with him during the school day, the Lord was going to be with him wherever he went, and he could be strong and courageous because of that. Even when he felt weak, he didn't have to be afraid because the Lord his God would never leave him.

In this short passage, just three verses long, God tells His people to be strong and courageous three times. Why? Because at the time of unrest for them, when what they had known for so long was changing, they needed to remember and be close to what was true and familiar.

They needed to be close to God. They needed to know they were loved. God was going to be with them. He was never going to leave them. He loved them, and that would never change.

We can be patient, strong, and courageous because the Lord our God is with us wherever we go.

EXTRA VERSES FOR STUDY OR PRAYER

Read about God's care for His people in the entire book of Joshua.

VERSE OF THE DAY

Haven't I commanded you: be strong and courageous? Do not be afraid or discouraged, for the Lord your God is with you wherever you go. —Joshua 1:9

PRAYER

Father, thank You for the way You take such good care of me and my family. When things feel different, when what we've known to be true changes, and when we wonder what will happen to us, remind us of how much we're loved and help us to trust You with what comes. In Jesus's name, amen.

THINK

PRAY

PRAISE

TO-DO   PRAYER LIST

QUESTIONS FOR DEEPER REFLECTION

1. Has there been a time in your life when things were uncertain and everything changed?

2. What is your safe place? When things feel upside down, is there somewhere you go that provides strength? How can you invite God into that space with you?

Day 28

THE LORD IS MERCIFUL

He has shown you, O mortal, what is good. And what does the Lord require of you? To act justly and to love mercy and to walk humbly with your God. —Micah 6:8 (NIV)

It's amazing to me how easy it is for God's people to forget all He's done for them.

During our time together in this prayer journal, I've shared that my oldest son went through a serious heartbreak and setback during his senior year of high school. Thankfully, after spending seven months in intense physical therapy and rehabilitation before returning to hitting and throwing programs, he was able to start his senior year of high school baseball. But at just seventeen years old, he lacks the life experience, perspective, or history with God that I do to process what happened from a spiritual perspective. He doesn't have countless stories about how God made a way for him or opened the right doors at just the right time. Apart from this specific incident, he can't look back and remember that time when his need was so great, with no answer in sight...but then God stepped in.

But I can.

As we helped our son process this setback and tried to help him trust God through it, I drew from my own remembrances of God's provision. I trust God more now than I did when I was his age because I've seen Him come through for me over and over again. Not always in the way I had hoped—and sometimes in a way I didn't like or want. But He has never let me down. I have countless examples

I can share of God doing something for me that I could never have done for myself. Things I couldn't have made happen if I'd tried.

But to my shame, I still fail to remember them at times.

I'm not sure why it's so easy for me to forget, but I do know that when I'm feeling anxious, impatient, scared, or unsure about my future, it's because I have not remembered the ways God has taken care of me and my family in the past. When our son first got hurt, I was overwhelmed by sadness and frustration. I just simply couldn't believe God would allow something like that to happen to him after all he had been through following his dream to play college baseball. In fact, I remember saying to both my husband and the Lord, "How can this be the end of his story? It just doesn't seem right!"

In my heart, I knew God wasn't done. Our son's story is far from over, but I took my eyes off of what I know about the God I serve and looked at the temporal, what I could see with my eyes, for a few days. Those days were filled with unrest, turmoil, and many tears.

SOMETHING TO THINK ABOUT

This is the exact situation God's people found themselves in when we read the book of Micah. Countless times after leaving Egypt, the Israelites had been given instructions to remember. Throughout the book of Exodus alone, Moses instructed them over and over to remember all that God had done. He talked about God's provision on an almost constant basis. In Micah 6:3–5 (ESV), God seems to be pleading with them to remember Him:

> O my people, what have I done to you? How have I wearied you? Answer me! For I brought you up from the land of Egypt and redeemed you from the house of slavery, and I sent before you Moses, Aaron, and Miriam. O my people, remember…that you may know the righteous acts of the Lord.

Even though God had done for them what they couldn't do for themselves, they forgot Him over and over again. And yet, God continued to show them mercy.

Mercy simply means compassion or forgiveness shown toward someone for whom it is within one's power to punish or harm. God certainly had the power to destroy the Israelites, and there were times when He *did* allow them to be punished and even harmed for their poor, sinful choices.

The baseball accident our son suffered was not a punishment for anything, but it was a difficult reminder that we are not in control of our own lives. At any time, God can redirect us or allow things that are challenging to enter our paths. But that's the power in remembering. It keeps us full of faith that what God once did, He can do again.

We can be patient because our God is full of mercy, showing compassion and forgiveness, and making a way for us even when we forget Him.

EXTRA VERSES FOR STUDY OR PRAYER

Deuteronomy 8

VERSE OF THE DAY

He has shown you, O mortal, what is good. And what does the Lord require of you? To act justly and to love mercy and to walk humbly with your God. —Micah 6:8 NIV

PRAYER

Father, thank You for being full of mercy. When I forget what You've done for me, You lovingly and gently remind me. You have given me Your Word, full of true stories that prove Your provision. Help me believe that what You once did, You can do again. In Jesus's name, amen.

THINK

PRAY

PRAISE

TO-DO   PRAYER LIST

QUESTIONS FOR DEEPER REFLECTION

1. Think of a time when you felt anxiety over an unknown future or a very challenging event. Now, intentionally bring to memory the things that God has done for you over the years. If you can't remember much, search the Scriptures to discover what God has done in the lives of others. Deuteronomy 8 is a good place to start.

2. When you choose to dwell on what God has done, what starts to shift in your emotions? What starts to change in the way you see what's happening around you?

Day 29

THE LORD IS STRONG

The LORD my LORD is my strength; he makes my feet like those of a deer and enables me to walk on mountain heights!
—Habakkuk 3:19

"My God is so big, so strong, and so mighty, there's nothing my God cannot do."

I taught my children this song, "My God Is So Big," when they were very young, straight from a VeggieTales sing-along CD. The memory of their little arms stretched wide as they demonstrated the bigness of God, making a muscle as they showed me His strength, and crossing back and forth as a sign that there was nothing their God could not do will forever be etched in my mama memory.

In their little years, I think they saw God as a superhero. My boys were obsessed with capes. There wasn't a day that went by that they didn't have a blanket tied around their necks. They even did homeschool lessons while wearing capes, and I never tried to change it. They wore capes to the grocery store, capes out to dinner, and capes at the kitchen table. It was one of those things I knew they would outgrow soon enough, so I left it alone. It's easy to see why it was so effortless for them to make the jump from the words of that VeggieTales song to what they believed about the God who created them.

I guess God is a kind of ultimate superhero, creating something from nothing, wiping out the world and starting over, parting oceans, causing great fish to swallow men and then spit them back out, and all of the other amazing things He has done. The biblical stories we focus on sharing with our kids make God seem larger than life—and

He is. He will be strong for us, maybe even in dramatic fashion like He was for Adam and Eve, Noah, Moses, and Jonah. But eventually, we need to see God as the hero of our small moments and not just the big, dramatic stories like those in the Bible.

The book *Hinds Feet on High Places*[17] is an allegory, revealing a hidden meaning. It's based on today's verse from Habakkuk 3:19. The story is meant to teach us about the ups and downs, difficulties and victories of walking an entire lifetime with Christ, maturing as we go.

Throughout the book, the main character, Much-Afraid, struggles to get her footing and trust the Lord as she encounters many scary and difficult things. In the beginning, she functions mainly in her own strength; over the course of the story, she must learn her own limitations and just how much she needs the King. There are some big, hairy, scary experiences she must survive, but there are also everyday inconveniences and relationship challenges she must learn to endure, all the while learning to trust that God can see from a vantage point—the highest of places—that she can't.

Once she reaches a certain level, Much-Afraid, now named Grace and Glory, looks back on all she's been through and all she's survived. She can now see so clearly where she's been, as if she's been given glasses and can see perfectly for the first time.

SOMETHING TO THINK ABOUT

In chapter 19, Grace and Glory and her handmaidens Joy and Peace spend several weeks exploring the heights and learning from the King:

It was now perfectly evident to them that there must be ranges upon ranges of which they had never dreamed while they were still down in the narrow valleys with their extraordinarily limited views. Sometimes, as she looked on the glorious panorama visible from these lowest slopes in the Kingdom of Love, she found herself blushing...They had

17. Hannah Hurnard, *Hinds' Feet on High Places* (Carol Stream, IL: Tyndale Momentum, 1979).

been able to see so little and were so unconscious of what lay beyond and above. If that had been the case while down in the valley, how much more clearly, she now realized, that even up on those wonderful slopes she was only looking on a tiny corner of the whole.[18]

God has equipped us all with a certain amount of strength. We all have different but equally valuable abilities to contribute to our own stories. We might even be the heroes of these stories for a time, but there will eventually come a day when we realize how much we need Jesus. We'll slip, fall, and have big, hairy, scary experiences that show us just how limited we are. But friends, this is a good thing. This will be the very best place for God to show us how big, strong, and mighty He is. Our strength will eventually fail, but God's never will. He will make us more and more like Him, giving us the ability to walk through whatever comes our way, big or small.

We can be patient because our God is so strong. He will be our strength when we have none, and we'll be better for it.

EXTRA VERSES FOR STUDY OR PRAYER

Second Corinthians 12:9; Ephesians 6:10

VERSE OF THE DAY

The Lord my Lord is my strength; he makes my feet like those of a deer and enables me to walk on mountain heights!
—Habakkuk 3:19

PRAYER

Father, I want to follow after You, and I always want to believe that You are my hero. To do that, I'll have to walk through some valleys, tripping and falling along the way. Help me to trust You to give me what I need to rise above all obstacles and walk the path You've chosen for me. In Jesus's name, amen.

---

18. Ibid.

THINK

_____

_____

PRAY

_____

_____

PRAISE

_____

_____

TO-DO   PRAYER LIST

_____

_____

_____

QUESTIONS FOR DEEPER REFLECTION

1. Do you find it harder to trust God in the big things, or in the small, everyday things?

_____

_____

2. Sometimes, I forget to trust God in the moments of my day, but these are the places where my faith often grows the most. What's one way you can invite God to be more involved in your everyday life?

_____

_____

Day 30

THE LORD IS COMING

If I go away and prepare a place for you, I will come again and take you to myself, so that where I am you may be also.

—John 14:3

Recently, my husband and I had front row seats as some close friends struggled with a coaching situation. In their opinion, their son wasn't getting the attention he deserved. According to them, he was overlooked and treated unfairly. All season long, the boy's father held back, doing his best to keep his mouth shut and let the coach be the coach. But after some time and many games had passed, his son said, "Dad, I want you to go to bat for me"—and our friend did just that.

For weeks, the son tried to handle the situation on his own. He did the best he could, but it never made a difference in the coach's treatment of him. Alone, he felt deflated and weak, but all of that changed when he knew his dad was coming to his aid.

There's something amazing about knowing your dad is coming.

As I write this, my own father is eighty-seven years old, and every moment I have with him is a gift. I treasure each holiday that he's with us and try my best to respect him, almost to a fault, because I want his last years on this earth to be filled with the knowledge that the people for whom he fought the hardest will fight for him in return. Over the years, my dad has come to my rescue more times than I could possibly count; he even did so just recently. He's been my confidant, my advisor, and the person I knew would stand with me no matter what. I've always known he was coming to my defense if I needed it. Even when

I didn't deserve it, he still came to my rescue. There has never been a time when I needed him that he wasn't there. And I know this season will end someday because that's just the way it goes.

Thankfully, I will still have the lessons Dad has taught me and the backing of my heavenly Father. That relationship can never be taken away, can never be dislodged, and it will never die.

In John 13, leading into John 14, Jesus is telling His disciples that His time is almost up. Soon, He'll be leaving them to return to heaven. They're troubled by this because they can't imagine functioning without Him, but He tells them not to be troubled.

> In my Father's house are many rooms. If it were not so, would I have told you that I am going to prepare a place for you? If I go away and prepare a place for you, I will come again and take you to myself, so that where I am you may be also.   (John 14:2–3)

There is tremendous peace in knowing that Jesus is coming back for us. God the Father will send His Son back for those He calls His own. He hasn't left us alone. He's simply gone to prepare a place for us. And while He's gone to heaven, we have the gift of the Holy Spirit to lead us, help us continue His ministry on earth, and "do even greater works than these" (John 14:12).

SOMETHING TO THINK ABOUT

We don't know when Jesus will return for us. (See Mark 13:32.)

We don't know where we will be when He returns. (See Luke 17:34–36.)

We pray that our family and friends will be among those for whom He returns...but we don't know for certain. (See Matthew 7:21–22.)

But we do know He's coming.

We can be patient, dear friends, because we serve the Lord who will come again and take us to be with Him in a place where "*death shall be no more, neither shall there be mourning, nor crying, nor pain anymore"* (Revelation 21:4 ESV).

We are only here for a season.

We're all just passing through.

EXTRA VERSES FOR STUDY OR PRAYER

Matthew 7:22; Mark 13:32; Luke 17:34–36; Revelation 21:4

VERSE OF THE DAY

If I go away and prepare a place for you, I will come again and take you to myself, so that where I am you may be also.

—John 14:3

PRAYER

Father, thank You for making it known that You will return. Thank You for giving Your children the confidence of knowing You are on Your way and that we have Your backing no matter what. We belong to You—and that changes everything. In Jesus's name, amen.

THINK

PRAY

PRAISE

TO-DO

_____

_____

_____

PRAYER LIST

_____

_____

_____

QUESTIONS FOR DEEPER REFLECTION

1. Do you think much about the strong support God offers You?

_____

_____

2. Can you allow God to be Your Father in the truest, richest meaning that this brings?

_____

_____

ABOUT THE AUTHOR

Brooke McGlothlin received her B.S. in psychology from Virginia Tech and her master's degree in counseling from Liberty University. For over ten years, she served as director of clinical services in a local pregnancy care ministry before making the best choice of her life— to stay home with her boys. Brooke uses her ministry experience to reach women, writing to bring hope to the messes of life in the midst of her own messy life.

In 2010, Brooke cofounded Raising Boys Ministries with Erin Mohring and equipped parents of boys to raise godly men for over nine years. In 2019, they launched a new ministry, Million Praying Moms, which exists to help moms make prayer their first and best response to the challenges of parenting.

Brooke now leads Million Praying Moms solo and hosts the Million Praying Moms podcast. You can find her writing and creating prayer resources for today's Christian moms at the Million Praying Moms blog. Among her books are *Everyday Prayers for Peace: A 30-Day Devotional & Reflective Journal for Women*; *Praying for Boys: Asking God for the Things They Need Most*; *Unraveled: Hope for the Mom at the End of Her Rope*; and *Praying Mom: Making Prayer the First and Best Response to Motherhood*.

Brooke, her husband, and their two sons make their home in the mountains of Appalachia, calling southwestern Virginia home.

To connect with Brooke, visit:

www.millionprayingmoms.com

www.brookemcglothlin.net